AT HOME AND AT WORK

Published in cooperation with the
NATIONAL COUNCIL ON FAMILY RELATIONS

Series Editor: **John Scanzoni**
Family Research Center
University of North Carolina, Greensboro

Books appearing in New Perspectives on Family are either single or
multiple-authored volumes or concisely edited books of original
articles on focused topics within the broad field of marriage and family.
Books can be reports of significant research, innovations in methodology,
treatises on family theory, or syntheses of current knowledge in a
subfield of the discipline. Each volume meets the highest academic
standards and makes a substantial contribution to our knowledge of
marriage and family.

Other volumes currently available from Sage and sponsored by NCFR:

AT HOME AND AT WORK

The Family's Allocation of Labor

Michael Geerken

and

Walter R. Gove

Published in cooperation with the
National Council on Family Relations

SAGE PUBLICATIONS
Beverly Hills / London / New Delhi

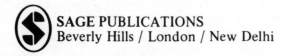

For information address:

SAGE Publications, Inc.
275 South Beverly Drive
Beverly Hills, California 90212

SAGE Publications India Pvt. Ltd.
C-236 Defence Colony
New Delhi 110 024, India

SAGE Publications Ltd
28 Banner Street
London EC1Y 8QE, England

Printed in the United States of America

Library of Congress Cataloging in Publication Data

Geerken, Michael.
    At home and at work.

    (New perspectives on family)
    Bibliography: p.
    1. Family research. 2. Wives—Employment—Social
aspects. 3. Husband and wife. 4. Sex role. 5. Home
economics. 6. Division of labor. I. Gove, Walter R.
II. National Council on Family Relations. III. Title.
IV. Series.
HQ728.G34   1982   306.8'7   82-21467
ISBN 0-8039-1940-9
ISBN 0-8039-1941-7 (pbk.)

FIRST PRINTING

Contents

Series Editor's Foreword

In their 1980 *Journal of Marriage and Family* decade review article, Holman and Burr suggest that functionalism as a way of doing family studies has in recent years become virtually nonexistent. Professors Geerken and Gove are attempting to "strip away" some of functionalism's serious shortcomings, and then to combine it with certain perspectives from microeconomic theory in order to help explain the work patterns of married women, the household task performance of both spouses, and finally, selected aspects of marital quality.

Not everyone will agree with the theoretical assumptions made by the authors, the ways in which they carry out their work, their conclusions, and in particular their implicit hints that their approach is relatively value-free by comparison to those of some feminists and other advocates of family change.

Nevertheless, they have produced a well-crafted piece of research, and their point of view deserves a hearing in the NCFR-Sage Series. Our goal is to present a variety of perspectives in theory, research, policy, and application. Certainly most researchers and clinicians will agree with their suggestion on the book's final page that future research into these complex matters should focus on the actual decision-making processes resulting in household chore and employment outcomes.

—John Scanzoni

1

Theories of
the Family

HISTORICAL PERSPECTIVES
AND CURRENT APPROACH

The sharp increase in the number of working wives in
recent years has led to a growing interest in the family's allocation
of labor, especially on the part of sociologists and economists.
Approaching the phenomenon from different perspectives, the
two disciplines have nonetheless shown a common interest
in why more wives are going to work outside the home and
how this changes the distribution of housework among family
members.

For a better understanding of the dynamics of work/house-
work allocation within the nuclear family, we will bring together
common lines of thought in sociology and economics in order to
develop a unified theory of work allocation based on the notion
of "utility maximization" by the family unit. By utility maximization, we mean that people strive to make themselves as
happy as possible given limited resources. Utility, as we use it,
encompasses both monetary and nonmonetary endeavors (Armen, 1969; Gram, 1975). After an empirical test of the theory
based on data from a recent national sample, we examine the
effect of various forms of work allocation under different conditions by measuring the impact of different allocation schemes
on the quality and viability of marriages.

An explicit concern with the internal structure of the family
and how that structure interacts with the larger society can be
roughly dated from the rise of the "structural-functionalist"
school during the forties and fifties, a school that emphasized

the structure of society and its institutions. Until then, most scientific research on the family was from an "interactionist" approach that focused on individuals and was strongly influenced by the work of symbolic interactionists and by certain psychoanalytic concepts (Hill and Hansen, 1960). More recent developments have taken a microscopic approach, although they now incorporate a concern with structure and with the relationship between structures in the family and society.

In the early 1920s the interactionist perspective shifted away from its reform orientation and concern with the problems of the lower-class family to an emphasis on the characteristics and dynamics of the middle-class family. More concerned with the "scientific" study of the family than with reform of the slums, researchers conceived of the family less in terms of its structure than of the interaction among the personalities of its members (Burgess, 1926). A mass of literature was generated by psychiatry, social work, and other professions with similar "personal adjustment" orientations.

The interactionist approach to the family was a dynamic one, with personal interaction treated as a continuous internal process. Action was the result of communication processes, and family phenomena were interpreted with reference to role playing, status relations, communication problems, decision making, stress reactions, and socialization processes. The family was treated primarily as a closed system. The focus was more on individual adjustment and happiness than on the stability of the marital bond itself (Schvaneveldt, 1966). An extensive literature has accumulated in this vein, but there has been very little systematic theory building or conscious evolution of a testable set of hypotheses to organize and suggest research (Burr et al., 1979). Though in sociology other perspectives grew and surpassed the interactionist approach in popularity after World War II, the interactionist approach, broadly defined, is still characteristic of much of the present work on the family outside sociology, anthropology, and economics, and much of the work of sociologists themselves still runs in this direction.

The Depression and World War II provided strong evidence of the importance of the larger socioeconomic system to individual adjustment and happiness. As a result, an increased emphasis on the structure of society and the interaction of its institutions appeared in the structural-functionalist school in the late forties and early fifties, led by Talcott Parsons. It was in some ways a return to the macroscopic concerns of the social Darwinists of the late nineteenth century, particularly their interest in the place of the family in man's development. Yet a whole new set of questions was being asked, centered around the structure of society and the family, and the important linkages of the family to the social system as a whole.

The central purpose of the structural-functionalist approach was to explain the existence and nature of the family relationship by reference to the needs of the social system as a whole. Special attention was given to the changes in family structure mandated by the industrialization of society, such as a shift to a smaller, or nuclear, rather than an extended family (Parsons, 1943). A modern industrialized society, it was proposed, was best served by a sex-based division of labor. This division of labor assigned the role of the economic provider to the husband, who was to see to the *instrumental* needs of the family, such as food and shelter, while the nonworking housewife functioned in an *expressive* role oriented to the emotional needs of the family members (Parsons and Bales, 1955). Some elaborations of this approach suggested that the Western "love and marriage" ideology functioned to provide women not directly involved in the economic structure with a link to the structure through their husband's occupations, and to justify the procreation of children, which was considered economically irrational for an individual but obviously vital to the long-term maintenance of the social system (Greenfield, 1966).

With these basic trends in mind, we should now explore some underlying concepts. Merton (1957: 52) and others have said that the explanation of an institution, structure, or process as "functional" requires a referent—a specification of the system or organism for which that element is functional. Bell and Vogel (1960) make this point specifically about the structural-functional approach to the family.

The functional framework for family analysis originally emphasized the *societal* function. That is, the nature of family roles was explained in terms of the purpose they served in maintaining a viable social structure. But family structure may be functional for other systems, and the notion of functional referent can be a very complex question. In fact, at least three referents and their corresponding types of functional analysis have been identified. The first, defined by Hill and Hansen (1960), can be termed *macrofunctionalism*—it is concerned with the needs that the family and its structure fulfill for the socioeconomic system of the society. Its functional referent is thus society as a whole. The other two are both classified as *microfunctional:* (a) analysis of how the family structure serves to maintain the family unit itself (the family itself is the functional referent), and (b) analysis of how the needs of the individual family members are served by the family structure. In the latter, the functional referent is the individual (particularly his or her personality and happiness).

These three forms of family functional analysis are clearly analytically separable. Society, the family, and the individual can each be described as a system that has its own boundaries but interacts with other systems (if we characterize the human personality as a system), and each can thus operate with its own logic at least partly independent of the needs of the other two. Though theoretically only the individual actually makes rational choices, both family and society can make demands that ignore certain basic individual needs. An individual family member can make choices that, at least in the short run, are profitable for the family unit (its stability and viability) but not for the person as an individual. The social system also has its own relentless processes, and if it is to survive, it must reward behaviors that reinforce it and negatively sanction or ignore behaviors that do not.

Nevertheless, often a structure simultaneously fulfills the needs of all three systems (society, family, and individual).

Indeed, this must be generally true if a stable society is to exist at all. The more a family's structure meshes with both individual personalities and the needs of the socioeconomic system, the smoother all three are likely to run. But our modern industrial society is constantly changing, and there are always discontinuities, dysfunctions, and frictions—so that in some cases the needs of the larger society, the family unit, and the individual do differ. The friction among these systems is not a theoretical problem to be defined away, but an important phenomenon to be investigated. The best vantage point for such an investigation is the center—the structure of the family.

The present analysis takes from the structural-functionalist perspective two important ideas. First, any study of family structure must take into account the linkages between the external society and the family (Scanzoni, 1970). The family does not exist in a vacuum, and its continuation depends in part on the extent to which that structure is likely to be rewarded (both in economic and social goods) by the social system. Second, the specification of *functional referent* is important. Some conditions in the economic system can be functional for the individual's well-being, but not for the marriage. And some types of family structure are not functional, either for the external socioeconomic system or the individual personality systems. These are, of course, likely to be short-lived, but they can exist through habit or cultural lag. There is some evidence, for example, that when an extended family lives together, it poses a strain on the marital bond and has a negative impact on the psychological well-being of the individual (Gove et al., 1983). We will remain aware of the issue of multiple functional referents, but our focus will be the importance of family structure for the family itself.

The *functionality* of a family structure for the family unit can be defined simply as the contribution (positive or negative) that the structure makes to keeping the marriage stable and viable. The explanation must include, of course, how the family structure adapts to the larger social system and to its own internal composition. Family structure will therefore be treated primarily as a dependent variable relative to the external system, and as an independent variable—given the conditions imposed by the larger society—with regard to the quality of the marital relationship. It is also both possible and useful to study opposite effects, such as the impact of family structure on the larger social system (see Bell and Vogel, 1960: 8-19, for a review of some of this research). Since, over the short run, most effects probably operate *from* the external *to* the family system, and since the cross-sectional survey used in this study is best suited to short-term effects, the family will be treated more as reacting to rather than on the larger socioeconomic structure.

"Family structure" can refer to many patterns of interac tion, including typical decision-making processes, accepted methods of child rearing, patterns of kinship contact, and patterns of sexual relations over time. The subject matter of this book concerns one of the most important of the many identifiable family structures: *work/housework role allocation*—the allocation of both income-producing work (generally outside the home) and household tasks (including child care) among family members. The focus will be on the nuclear family—the husband and wife together with their children. The outlines of this study are similar to those recently proposed by Pleck and Nichols (1977), who concentrated on what he called the "work-family role systems." This analysis differs from his only in its specific concern with the allocation of labor (within and outside the home) among the family members.

The notion of "role," both as it is used by Pleck and as it will be used occasionally here, must be differentiated from its more formal use in recent work by such researchers as Nye (1976). The traditional use of the term "role" relates to the notion of "status" or position in the social structure. A role is simply the set of cultural expectations attached to a position. Another use of the term, popular among social psychologists, is that a role is simply the "typical behavior of persons occupying a status (position) which, in fact, either validates the cultural expectations or emerges to create new roles" (Nye and Gecas, 1976: 6). A role, then, may be a cultural norm for a position or simply a set of behaviors associated with a position. This analysis will not be framed in the terms of the first definition, since our focus is not as much on society as on the family. Cultural expectations concerning role behavior will be treated as one aspect of the socioeconomic structure to which the family must adapt. To be sure, the commitment of family members to cultural norms concerning family role behavior must be included in any analysis of work/housework allocation—but only as one relevant factor among many.

We focus, then, on the way labor is allocated among family members, with the assumption that the allocation is fairly stable over the short run—that is, the same family member tends to do the same tasks most of the time, until and unless there is a change in family circumstances. This focus is chosen for a number of reasons. First, the outside job is the most important link between the family and the external economic system, and largely determines the social status and quality of life of the family members. Second, the work/housework allocation is the most important determinant of the individual family member's day-to-day experience of time and energy demands. Third, the external system's effects on work role allocation (especially labor force participation of the wife) and on the household division of labor have already received a great amount of attention, especially in the last decade, and are at the center of the current debates about the nature of sex roles. Finally, this structure is the easiest to define and the most reliable of family structures to measure in a survey, since it is concrete and less subject to being distorted in an interview than, for example, the decision-making structure of the family.

In our conceptual framework, work/housework role structure will be treated as evolving in response to (1) external pressures of the society and (2) internal demands created by the number of children and their ages. Remember, however, that the links between family members and these two systems depend at least partly on the characteristics of the members themselves.

Sociologists interested in work/housework role structure rightly tend to concentrate on variables such as family income, wife's education, and family size and their relationships to household task allocation and the labor force participation of the wife. Yet there is no overall theory of task allocation, none that connects known relationships in a logical way and points to new areas of investigation.

Economists, on the other hand, especially since the seminal works of Mincer (1962) and Becker (1965), have been much more successful in evolving a general theory of household task allocation because they are willing to make certain essential assumptions. They approach the household unit's relation to internal and external contingencies under the assumption that the household will always try to do its best to function as well as it can. Though economists are not generally aware of it, such an assumption is substantially equivalent to the approach in sociology that attempts to explain family structures in terms of their contribution to the life of the family unit itself. It does not do substantial violence to either framework to characterize them as essentially similar in at least one sense: Both suppose that the explanation for the relationship between the external system and internal family structure lies in the family unit's tendency to "do the best it can under the circumstances." The family "maximizes its utility" under whatever conditions it finds itself; therefore, its structure can be explained in terms of that structure's "functionality" for the family itself.

In sum, the conceptual framework developed here makes use of theoretical contributions from both sociologists and economists. The focus on the allocation of labor both outside and inside the household requires study of attempts to explain the decision to work outside the home, the allocation of tasks inside the home, and the relationship between the two. Until recently, research and theory on the family and the world of paid labor have tended to treat the two arenas as two different systems. This has been termed "the myth of separate worlds" (Kantor and Lehr, 1975). In economics, the treatment of labor supply and other work-related topics rarely came into contact with "home economics," considered to be a field having little to do with economic theory. In sociology, the separation of the two worlds was made explicit. Parsonian theory (Parsons, 1949) held that occupational life was organized around impersonal standards of competence linked to the technical content of a function, whereas the family was the place of custom, particularistic concerns of the individual, and emotional expression. Work served an instrumental function, family an expressive function.

A review of the relevant theory and research shows that economists have done the key theoretical work on jobs outside the home in their theories of labor supply and time allocation. Family sociologists have done more work on household tasks, though no overall theory of task allocation has been evolved, and more attention has been paid to an individual's power than to task performance. The following review of research and theory on the determinants of work/housework role allocation thus tends to emphasize the economic approach to labor supply and time allocation, and to emphasize sociological research on the nature of the division of labor within the household and on the effects of idoelogy on that allocation system.

ROLE STRUCTURE AS UTILITY MAXIMIZATION

The economic research relevant to the work/housework role structure has been generated largely by a concern with labor supply theory as it applied to married women (see especially Mincer, 1962). This theoretical approach was generalized by the time-allocation theory of Becker (1965) to include the "nonmarket productive" activities of married women. The model was further tested and refined by Cain (1966) and especially by Bowen and Finegan (1969). Leibowitz (1975) elaborated the theory as it applies to the division of household labor.

The traditional economic theory of labor supply focuses on the husband. The household is treated as a unit, and the explanation of labor supply centers around the effects of wage rate on the decision to work. In the classical theory of labor supply, all time is conceived of as divided between work and leisure, with an increase in one implying an equal decrease in the other. Two contradictory effects of wage rate have been identified: the *wage* effect (sometimes called the *income* effect) and the *substitution* effect (also called the *price* effect). The wage effect means that wage rate has a negative impact on hours spent in marketwork—the more you're paid, the less you'll work. This occurs because an increase in wages is assumed to cause an increase in consumption of all goods, including leisure. Leisure is thus treated as a consumable "good." The second effect is contradictory to the former; the substitution effect is based on the notion of "opportunity cost" and operates in the following way: An increase in the wage rate for marketwork increses the "price" or opportunity cost of leisure, because the marketwork foregone becomes more valuable. You lose more by foregoing marketwork if you are paid more—that is, the "price" of leisure goes up as the value of work goes up.

This classical theory, however, was found to be an unsuitable model of women's labor force participation. As we have pointed out, classical labor supply theorists assumed that for all practical purposes, men made up the labor force, or at least that a household could be treated as a single worker. Furthermore, it was assumed that there were only two kinds of activity—marketwork and leisure. These assumptions were based on the idea that women, particularly married women, did not work in occupations or in numbers that had a significant impact on the economy. Housework did not constitute real "labor" and, in any case, men did not do housework. A very similar group of attitudes, of course, was present among structural-functionalist sociologists, who conceived of women's family role as "expressive" and emotional, and thus not constituting "true" work.

Such approaches were made obsolete by the increase in the number of married women in the labor force during and after World War II (Lloyd, 1975). Especially in economics, there was an increasing interest in the labor force activity of women. Because of the obvious involvement of women in housework, however, the theories of labor supply and time allocation grew to include a three-way option for women in the division of their time into marketwork, nonmarketwork, and leisure. Husbands were still assumed to choose only between paid labor and leisure.

Classical labor supply theory has been applied to women in an important study by Mincer (1962). He suggests that the demand for leisure is an inadequate explanation for women's labor supply, and that the "demand for housework" must also be included. He postulates that it is the *relative* productivity of marketwork as opposed to nonmarketwork that determines the labor force participation of females, and that this relative productivity is a function of the potential market productivity of both the husband and wife. Thus, an increase in total family income creates an increase not only in the demand for leisure, but in the demand for "home goods" as well. If the husband's productivity in the market exceeds his wife's, the greater his income, the greater will be the family's consumption of leisure and home goods. His wife will then be needed more for work at home, since her time there will be "cheaper" than his.

In Mincer's early formulation, the family acts as a *unit* in choosing the wife's degree of involvement in marketwork. It is the family's well-being (consumption of goods and leisure) that governs the choice, rather than the desires of the husband or wife alone: "The decisions about the production of goods and services are largely family decisions. . . . An increase in one individual income may not result in a decrease in *his* hours of work, but in those of other family members" (Mincer, 1962: 66).

Mincer adds that the distribution of leisure, marketwork, and housework among family members is governed also by "tastes" (a catch-all phrase for individual preferences) and by "biological or cultural specification of function." It is clear that such a framework fits neatly into the structural-functional approach in sociology: Family role allocation is functional for the family unit as a whole. The household, rather than the individual, is the focus of attention.

After testing his model with a number of different data sets, Mincer concluded that wives' labor force participation responds negatively to husband's income and positively to wife's earning power, and that the second effect is about twice as strong. He also found that wives' choice of outside work responds more strongly to "transitory" income than permanent income. This is easiest to describe in the extreme case. If the husband is, for example, temporarily unemployed, the wife is apt to take a job to preserve the family's standard of living rather than adjust that living standard downward. Her labor force participation will be greater than that of a woman whose husband is chronically unemployed (whose family thus has a lower "permanent income"). Further, if the head of a household is over 35, the higher his or her educational level, the weaker the effect of income on labor force participation because of accumulated assets.

In an expansion of Mincer's approach, Cain (1966) includes a direct measure of the demand for home goods (rather than one deduced from family income) by considering the number of children in his model. Together with the wife's "home skills," this variable makes up the "home wage of the wife" (1966: 8).

Bowen and Finegan (1969) present a greatly expanded analysis of female labor force participation. Notable findings include the independent effect of husband's employment status and the powerful effect of the presence of children and age of youngest child. (Number of children was not included.) They also introduced explicit consideration of the competition of women's labor markets.

In relating work/housework role structure to the larger society, then, these microeconomists hold that the articulation of husband's and wife's roles depends on the potential relative productivities of husband and wife in both the external economic and the internal family system. Potential productivities are indicated largely by the wage rates of husband and wife (either real or deduced from a measure like education) and the demand for household services. Husband and wife take the roles best suited for the family's well-being by allocating roles based on their relative productivities. The driving force behind those choices is the optimization of the family's utility.

The chief criticism leveled at these approaches (see, for example, Lloyd, 1975; Pleck and Nichols, 1977) is that they all ignore husband's nonmarketwork in their formulations.

Men are seen as making decisions concerning their occupation, employment status, and income, while women respond to these decisions in light of their own relative productivity, family needs, the availability of substitutes (goods for services—such as automatic dishwashers—or services for services—such as hired help), and the competition in female job markets. Men allocate their time between leisure and work; women must also do housework.

THE SOCIOLOGICAL APPROACH

Historically, economists have focused primarily on paid labor supply and the labor force participation of men and women—that is, on the allocation of marketwork among household members. Household chores are introduced theoretically because they are necessary to complete the picture of women's labor supply, but there has been as yet only one empirical test of time allocation by an economist using housework data (see Leibowitz, 1975). Until recently, family sociologists have been the researchers primarily interested in the household division of labor, its causes and effects.

Housework allocation varies in the degree to which it is shared, both in terms of individual tasks and of the total volume of activity. Housework also varies in *total* amount of work done (or time spent) by any family member. For example, it is possible for a housewife to do all the work in her home and still do less housework than another woman who receives a lot of help from her husband but whose household simply requires more work.

Most research in the division of household labor relates task allocation either to the wife's employment status or to household composition. In analyses of a 1955 Detroit sample, Blood and Wolfe (1960) found that when wives were employed, their husbands performed a greater proportion of the household work (not including child care), even with crude controls for husband's income. Other studies (Hoffman, 1963; Blood and Hamblin, 1958) concur that husbands help more if wives work. This has also been found in studies of "dual-career" families

(Poloma, 1970; Poloma and Garland, 1971; Rapoport and Rapoport, 1971).

In contrast, time budget studies (Walker and Gauger, 1970; Meissner et al., 1975; Robinson, 1977; Szalai, 1975; Gronau, 1976, 1977; Gove and Peterson, 1980; Berk and Berk, 1979) generally find that husbands show no increase in total time spent on household tasks when their wives work. The one exception to this finding is that they do show a slight increase when a young child is present. Wives, however, show a sharp drop in their time spent in housework when they work outside the home.

Though it is clear that household task allocation is more egalitarian for working than nonworking women—especially mothers—all evidence shows clearly that women still do the bulk of housework. Household tasks are largely differentiated by sex (Blood and Wolfe, 1960; Gove and Peterson, 1980), and women still do most of them. Some evidence indicates that husbands respond to wives' employment more in some tasks than in others, especially regarding child care (Oakley, 1974; Gove and Peterson, 1980), but the time budget studies show that this does not change total time spent by husbands.

Available evidence shows that children increase the wife's share of most household chores, and this share rises steadily with number of children until the fourth child (Campbell, 1970). A drop after that is largely the result of help from teenage children. Walker (1969), for example, found that up to 30 percent of housework is performed by children when no younger children are present. As the number of children increases, so does total task differentiation between spouses, with more tasks performed unilaterally by each (Blood and Wolfe, 1960). The evidence is clear that both the number and ages of children have an impact on household task allocation.

Most research on the division of household labor concerns the effect of wife's employment status and, to a lesser extent, that of the number and ages of children. It is clear, however, that other variables, particularly the relative social and economic resources of husband and wife apart from their employment status (for example, income and education), should also be included in any model of household division of labor. This follows from the time-allocation models of the economists and has also been suggested by sociologists (see, for example, Blood, 1963; Kantor and Lehr, 1975; Pleck and Nichols, 1977).

The effect of education of both husband and wife on task allocation has been investigated by a few researchers. As Farkas (1975) indicates, the effect of education on division of labor can be given a "narrow sociological" interpretation in which it is seen as a proxy for ideology or "tastes" concerning the proper allocation of housework between husband and wife. Using a panel design, he found that the greater the wife's education relative to the husband's, the more tasks are shared (hours of housework engaged in by husband, hours of marketwork by wife, and frequency of years in which some of both occurred). Similarly, he found greater task sharing, the more similar the wife's income was to the husband's. Nevertheless, the strongest determinants of specialization are family size and age of youngest child. Though he interprets his analysis as a comparison of a "narrow economic" versus a "narrow sociological" approach, it is clear that the economists properly consider both education and number and ages of children in their formulations. Leibowitz (1975), for example, uses wife's education to weave a quite detailed, theoretical elaboration of time-allocation theory as applied to wife's allocation *among* household tasks. Using a reanalysis of Walker and Gauger's (1970) time budget data, as well as other studies, she found that a wife's education negatively affects time spent on all household activities except child rearing, for which there is a positive effect. She shows how this result fits neatly with the economic model. Her analysis is considerably weakened, however, by the fact that she fails to control for wife's participation in outside work.

More "sociological" variables have also been related to household division of labor. Occupational prestige, both of husband and wife, is expected to influence task distribution in much the same way as income increases the value of time for economists. Hesselbart (1976) found that the wife's occupational prestige negatively affects her degree of household task participation, but that husband's occupation has virtually no effect. Scanzoni (1970) ties the prestige of the husband's occupation to marital satisfaction, but unfortunately his theory is an instrumental-expressive formulation and assumes a priori that the family derives its status and ultimate satisfaction through the husband's work.

Many researchers point to the importance of traditional norms, primarily sex roles, in the division of tasks. Most assume, in fact, that this is the primary cause of the division of labor in the United States. There have been few good studies measuring the actual effect that sex role ideology has on behavior in Western industrial culture. As Hesselbart (1976) points out, most studies either do not actually present relationships concerning attitudes and behavior (most use only college samples) or include only a few attitude items. Her own study with a better sample found that items related to traditional family values or male dominance do show moderate relationships with traditional sex-role behavior, even controlling for class resources and life-cycle variables. Global, generalized measures of egalitarianism, however, show no relationships.

The evidence from both economic and sociological studies indicates that a variety of factors must be taken into account in the prediction of family work/housework allocation. The economic theories of labor supply and time allocation indicate that the income and education of both husband and wife jointly determine the productivity of each in the market sector. The massive sociological research on occupational prestige justifies its inclusion in the model. Though a husband's occupation has long been assumed to be the measure of the family's status, as well as his own, recent evidence indicates that the wife obtains status from her own occupation as well as that of her husband, and that the status of her occupation has effects on a range of family variables independent of her husband's occupation (Barth and Watson, 1967; Ritter and Hargens,

1975; Rossi et al., 1974; Philliber and Hiller, 1978). Haug (1973) demonstrated that in many couples the occupational and educational level of the wife exceeds that of her husband, and so family social class measures based only on husband's income, occupation, and/or education contain a good deal of error just on that account. Clearly, then, any analysis of the relative market productivities of husband and wife must take into account the income, education, and occupational status of both.

As Mincer (1962) has pointed out, not just the demand for leisure based on the value of marketwork, but also the demand for housework must be included in any model of work/housework allocation. Economic studies show that the stage in the family's life cycle, as determined by the presence, number, and ages of children, is by far the most important determinant of the need for housework. Demands created by children include not only extra time spent on child care itself, but also time for laundry and dishes, meal preparation, transportation, house cleaning, and other tasks. The family life cycle is an excellent predictor of the wife's work involvement both inside and outside the home.

At the beginning of this chapter, we proposed that the family work/housework allocation system evolved in response to the larger socioeconomic system. A review of the relevant economic and sociological research has provided a picture of the relationship between family task allocation and the larger system. According to economists, the involvement of husband and wife in outside jobs and household tasks is based on their relative productivities in these two worlds and on the family's needs. Market productivities are best determined by the income and education of both husband and wife. Family composition and life-cycle stage are the most important determinants of inner structural demands. Sociologists define certain other connections of family members to the external system. Occupational prestige is added to education and income as a measure of a working family member's "value" to his or her family. "Status" is both a personal resource and a resource conferable on the family unit itself. It is a measure of productivity in the "social market.".The family is also tied into the larger social structure through the values it absorbs from the culture. Family task allocation is thus in part a response to societal traditions concerning the "proper" mode of task allocation, particularly the sexual division of labor. The family is thus tied into the larger socioeconomic structure through the education, income, and occupational prestige of its members, as well as its contact with societal norms governing behavior.

But what is the nature of the family's response to its environment? The microeconomists assume that the family responds in a rational, utility-maximizing way and derive their models from that assumption. The structural-functionalists also perceive family structure as a need-filling response to contingencies. But any empirical analysis shows that in practice there seems to be a *range* of family structural responses to similar sets of contingencies. Not everyone (or every family) responds in the same way under similar conditions. When any model based on the assumption that families maximize utility is applied to real data, there is error. Much of the error is not in the assumption itself, but simply in the fact that more theoretical specification is necessary when applying that assumption to data from a complex world. There is another possibility, however. Though it might be true that the typical family response to structural contingencies is "rational," the responses of many families may not be. Some families may simply make bad choices.

In a recent work, Harvey Leibenstein (1976) introduced some ideas relevant to the assumption that households "maximize utility." Microeconomists concerned with the family tend to treat the family in about the same way they treat the *firm* acting in a *market*. The firm is generally assumed to be profit-maximizing, and any inefficiencies of production and consumption are seen to be problems of the market itself (for example, monopoly relationships). Similarly, the family optimizes its utility as a unit. Leibenstein, however, proposes that we discard the assumption that the "firm" is necessarily profit-maximizing. He believes that more inefficiency in a real market occurs inside rather than outside the firm. In fact, firms might be rated according to their profit-maximization behavior, and this rating he terms their "X-efficiency."

This concept of "X-efficiency" might be measured as the success or viability of a given work-allocation structure under the conditions imposed by internal and external contingencies. When applied to the connection of external and internal structures discussed earlier, such an approach implies that the evolved response of family role structure to the external system is only partly rational. Many other factors such as habit and inertia, misperception of contingencies, and even stupidity also enter into the choice of a family's work/housework structure. In addition, "selective rationality," another useful concept introduced by Leibenstein, plays a part. To make a rational choice involves an expenditure of time and energy. It therefore involves costs. Rationality is employed selectively, and other criteria—ideology, habit, the opinions of others—will sometimes determine a decision instead.

This assumption of imperfect profit maximization implies that for any given set of conditions, there will appear a range of solutions—some better than others, some equally good—employed by the family (firm). In fact, it may be a mistake to assume that either the most frequently chosen or the "average" role structure is necessarily the best, since the distribution of role structures may be just beginning to change in response to conditions that have *already* changed in the external system. Such a lag may be caused by any of the factors suggested above, such as habit, inappropriate ideology, or false consciousness. Misperceptions also may occur because different elements of the external system change at different rates, and contradictory demands may be imposed simultaneously on a family by the external system.

But if we reject the notion that the typical family role structure under a given set of conditions is necessarily the best, are we left with *identifying* the typical structure? Not necessarily, because it is possible to measure the *viability* directly (and, by implication, the "functionality") of a form of family role structure by measuring the *potential for stability* that the structure creates for the family.

The way to measure this "potential for stability" is to measure the nature of the marital relationship and the feelings of the husband and wife about the marriage. Since we wish to focus on work/housework-allocation functions *for the marriage,* measures of individual happiness or well-being are inappropriate. The functionality of the family role structure is indicated by the healthy maintenance of the family unit (prevention of the "death" of the unit through divorce, separation, or annulment), and so works for the individual only to the extent that the role structure encourages that individual to maintain the relationship. Thus, our concern is with the quality and well-being of the family unit rather than the individual.

Such an approach not only allows us to identify clearly the forms of family role structure that are most beneficial in terms of the maintenance of the family unit, but also, and even more important, it allows for a different kind of analysis, one treating the relationship of an individual's happiness, well-being, and mental health to the proper functioning of his or her marriage as an empirical question. This kind of analysis is a complex question and deserves separate treatment, so it is not taken up here. Such analysis is not only compatible with but an important elaboration of the approach used here.

In this way the concerns of the interactional approach to family study can be linked to the functional viewpoint. The interactionist's concern with individual adjustment in marriage, when narrowed to the feeling of the individual toward the marriage, can thus be used to determine empirically the functionality of various kinds of work/housework structures. The first stage of this analysis, therefore, will ask the question: "How does the family respond, in terms of its work/housework allocation, to external and internal structural demands?" The second stage asks: "Given these external and internal conditions, what are the consequences of those family structural responses for the viability of the family unit itself?"

The analysis is founded on two groups of assumptions:

(1) The work/housework role structure evolves in response to
    (a) structural demands imposed by the larger economic system in the form of material rewards and sanctions;

    (b) the special needs and problems encountered at each stage of the family life cycle, particularly the presence, number, and ages of children; and

    (c) the social system and its expectations regarding the sexual division of labor as perceived by family members.

(2) The quality and stability of the marital relationship is strongly affected by the work/housework role structure through

    (a) the demands imposed and opportunities offered by the larger socioeconomic system; and

    (b) the demands created by the stage in the family life cycle.

The actual analysis of the data begins in the following chapter. Contrary to most other analyses, both by economists and sociologists, we have been able to include direct measurements of the allocation both of marketwork and housework in a single model of the determinants of the work/housework-allocation system. Such an approach presented some difficulties, however. For example, the wife's employment probably has a strong effect on household task allocation, so it is misleading to create a single variable that purports to measure the entire allocation system. It was therefore decided to break up the analysis into several parts. The first part concerns itself solely with the production of the labor force activity of wives. For both theoretical and statistical reasons, detailed analysis is performed only on that typical case in which the husband is employed. Variables of strictly economic interest (income, education) are combined with those of more specific interest to sociologists (occupational prestige, sex-role ideology) and with a measure of family life cycle in the model of female labor force participation.

Chapter 4 focuses on the household's division of labor, which is measured in two different ways. One measure concerns the sharing of household tasks. Other measures tap the actual time spent in household tasks by the husband and by the wife. This is the first time one study has looked at both kinds of measures, which some evidence indicates are to a certain extent independent of each other. Paralleling the earlier analysis of female labor force participation, detailed analysis using the same structural and ideological variables is performed for those cases in which (1) only the husband works outside the home and (2) both the husband and wife work outside the home.

The fourth chapter concludes this first stage of analysis, the determinants of family work/housework allocation. The second stage of the analysis, in Chapter 5, concerns the *effects* of work/ housework allocation on the viability of the family, which is operationalized by a variety of measures, including the closeness of the marital bond and the behaviors typical of the relationship. Since the effects are predicted to vary by the circumstances in which the family finds itself, various types of structures will be studied at various stages of the family life cycle and at different income levels—perhaps the two most important of the contingencies in which the family finds itself.

Chapter 6 contains a summary of findings and a discussion of needed future research.

2

Choice of Wife's Work Role

The past decade has seen a large number of empirical studies on the labor force activity of American women. The best multivariate analyses (Bowen and Finegan, 1969; Sweet, 1973) are based on data gathered in the 1960 census. Such comprehensive studies are not yet available for the 1970 census or for more recent years. The survey on which this monograph is based, though small (N = 1225) in comparison to such data sources as the 1/1000 census samples, is of sufficient size to test the general model described in the previous chapter. The main strength of this survey, however, lies in its measurement of the allocation of tasks both inside and outside the home, of attitudes of husband and wife toward the allocation system, and of the quality of the marital relationship itself.

Any survey using a national sample will, of course, yield less detailed and somewhat less accurate results than studies based on census data for those variables measured by both. This applies to the following analysis of labor force participation using our national survey data. The following analysis, however, (1) establishes a predictive model making use of concepts favored in economic analyses (such as income), as well as concepts favored in sociological theories of family role allocation (such as prestige and ideology); (2) demonstrates the applicability of previous census findings to our 1973 survey data, thereby providing support for the representativeness of the survey itself; and (3) establishes the model as a baseline for the study household task and time allocation to be performed in subsequent chapters.

THE DATA

During the winter of 1974-75, a probability sample of 2248 respondents aged 18 years and over and residing in the 48 contiguous states was interviewed under a grant from the National Science Foundation. The sampling, interviewing, and coding were done by Leiberman Research, Inc. The average interview lasted for one hour and twenty minutes. Besides the initial attempt to contact a potential respondent, two callbacks were made if no one was at home. Since the study was primarily designed to investigate the relationship between sex roles, marital roles, and mental health, the widowed and divorced (particularly males) were oversampled through the use of a stratified probability sample. The survey experienced an 8.8 percent refusal rate at the time of the screening interview and a 14.5 percent refusal rate (including breakoffs during the interview) after the household member to be interviewed had been randomly selected.

The following analyses will deal only with the married (N = 1225). Thus, the oversampling of the widowed and divorced will have no effect. The questionnaire was designed by the authors with the assistance of Claire Peterson. In an effort to identify clearly the nature of the married role and its psychological correlates, a substantial part of the questionnaire focused on measures of satisfaction with the marriage, the nature of the marital relationship, the allocation of household tasks, as well as demographic characteristics of both husband and wife. The questionnaire was designed to gather information relevant to a number of the key hypotheses found in the family and sex-role literature.

The independent variables can be summarized here for the entire monograph, because virtually the same general model is proposed to explain the allocation of both the marketwork and housework roles. The dependent variables will be discussed separately as they appear.

LINKAGES TO THE EXTERNAL SYSTEM

Income is the variable central to the economic approach to the family division of labor. Though other rewards are often included in economists' models, these rewards are either not measured or assumed to be included in other variables such as education or life-cycle stage.

Income is defined as that from all sources before taxes, including wages, pensions, insurance, inheritance, interest, unemployment compensation, welfare, and alimony and child support, in the past 12 months. The income of both respondent and spouse were orginally measured along a 21-category scale that was collapsed for the purposes of this analysis into five categories representing the best combination of frequency considerations (the attempt to obtain cells of reasonable size) and meaningfulness of categories. Because the incomes of husband and wife have very different distributions, it was necessary to collapse the categories differently for each to avoid an extremely skewed distribution in one or the other. Since the analysis treats each category as a dummy variable (see description of method following), this should not introduce bias into the procedure.

Occupational prestige is generally not considered in economists' representations of "productivity" vis-à-vis the larger economic system. It is often used by family sociologists, however, as a component of some kind of index of "social class" (see, for example, Scanzoni, 1970). Such an indexing procedure is not used here, since it is hypothesized that income, education, and occupational prestige all have independent effects on the family's work-allocation system. It is clear that the concept of occupational prestige (through which the job-holder confers a "status" on his or her family) should be included in any model where personal resources are important, but it is probably best included as a distinct predictor rather than as a component of an index.

Detailed census category occupational classifications were obtained from each respondent, and an 11-category classification system was used for his or her spouse. Each occupational category was assigned a prestige score based on those NORC prestige scores reported by Hodge et al. (1964). When more than one of NORC's occupational categories could be classified into one of the categories used in our survey, the median prestige score was assigned to our category. This introduced little error into the respondents' occupational classifications, because they were rather detailed, but the spouses' occupational classifications were rather general: professional, management/executive, small businessmen, salesman, clerical worker, skilled laborer/technician, semi-skilled laborer, unskilled laborer, other service occupation, public service worker, and other. These somewhat gross classifications (through better than the measurement of this variable in many studies) mean that for the spouse, the occupational prestige categories are somewhat less precise. Specifically, scores were found to be best collapsed into three categories with clear-cut gaps between them. "High" was a combination of professional and management/executive positions; "Medium" was composed of small businessmen, salesmen, clerical workers, and skilled laborer/technicians; and public service workers and the rest were classified as "Low." The few respondents in the "other" category were assigned to the three collapsed categories on the basis of their personal income and education.

Education is an important variable for both economists and sociologists interested in the division of family labor. For the nonworking wife, education is a proxy for her potential wage rate. It also has effects on the value and performance of housework, particularly child care (see, for example, Leibowitz, 1975). Most family economists assume that market wage is more elastic with respect to education than is housework productivity—that is, an increase in education produces a higher percentage increase in the potential productivity of marketwork than it does on the productivity of housework (the "nonmarketwork wage rate"). Thus, education is expected to have a positive effect on labor force participation (most evidence suggests that it does) and a negative effect on time spent in housework (the evidence is much weaker but provides some support).

Sociologists recognize the powerful effect of education on labor force participation, but also see it as a value in itself. It increases one's competency in many areas other than housework and paid labor. Perhaps more important, sociologists see education as a more important influence on sex-role ideology than other "class" variables (Farkas, 1975; Hesselbart, 1976) for both husband and wife. Its inclusion is therefore justified in these analyses on many different grounds and may be a richer measure of "productivity" or resources than those variables more closely tied to the job, such as income or occupational prestige.

Education was originally measured as an eight-category variable but was later collapsed into four categories: less than high school education, finished high school, some college, and completed college (4 years).

FAMILY COMPOSITION/LIFE CYCLE

The family life cycle has drawn increasing attention recently as the "developmental" approach to the family draws the interest of a growing number of researchers.

As it is usually used and as we will use it here, the family life cycle is defined chiefly by the presence, number, and ages of children living at home. Though much effort has gone into devising an ideal, detailed classification system for the life cycle (see the extensive discussion by Gove and Peterson, 1980), the more detailed the classification system, the larger the number of categories and hence the larger the sample size that is needed. The definition of the family life cycle used here deals with those characteristics of the family composition that have been found to have most relevance for work/housework structures in the past. These characteristics are number of children and age of youngest child living at home. In addition, couples who did not have children were classified as "prechild" if they had been married under seven years, "childless" if they had been married seven years or more and had never had children, and "empty nest" if they had children in the past, all of whom had left home or were over 18 years of age. Those couples who had children were cross-classified by the age of their youngest child (0-5, 6-17 years old) and by the number of children (1, 2-3, 4 or more). This design is used in Chapters 3 and 4. Such a scheme captures much of the variability in family life-cycle situations, while preserving sufficient cell sizes for reliable statistical analysis. (We focus more on age of youngest child in the present chapter for reasons which are explained below.)

Together, the three classes of variables presented here make up a "structural" model.[1] Husband, wife, and family are linked into the larger socioeconomic structure through their incomes, educational levels, and the prestige of their occupation. It is hypothesized that the nature of these connections to the larger structure at least partly determines the family's work/housework-allocation system. Stage in the family life cycle—defined largely by whether or not children are present or have been present, and if present, their number and ages—is a measure of *internal* structure. It is the combination of internal and external structural contingencies that makes up the structural model.

The dependent variable for all of the analyses in this chapter is wife's labor force participation, defined as a dichotomy: whether or not the wife was working (had paid employment) at the time of the survey. This approach to the allocation of the "work" (versus housework) role may be criticized on the grounds that the work status of both husband and wife should be simultaneously considered in any theory of work role allocation. This is a valid criticism, but employment status of the husband will not be considered here for a number of reasons. These reasons are less theoretical than they are practical and methodological.

The problems are both definitional and statistical. First, there is as yet no really viable role of "househusband" in American society. It can be assumed and supported with strong evidence that most unemployed men have not chosen the housekeeper role (Sobol, 1974). Though there is clearly structural and ideological discrimination against women in the job market, it is clear that the "unemployment" of the majority of nonworking married women involves more of a choice (their own or their family's) than does the unemployment of husbands of working age. The nonworking status (before retirement age) has a quite different meaning for men than for women. Our own survey supports this contention. Respondents were asked to specify their present employment status and that of their spouses. Nonworking respondents could classify themselves as "student," "retired," "keeping house," or "unemployed." In all, 21 non-working male respondents in our sample were not students or self-classified as retired. Of these, only 3 (14 percent) classified themselves as "keeping house." Of the 375 nonworking, non-retired, nonstudent females in our sample, 93.3 percent (350) classified themselves as "keeping house." Only 25 (6.7 per-cent) classified themselves as unemployed. The same dif-ference holds when one's spouse makes the designation. Only 9.5 percent of the female respondents with nonworking, non-retired, nonstudent husbands classified their spouses as "keep-ing house." The wife's comparable figure, as reported by their husbands, was 91 percent.

Husband's unemployment and wife's nonemployment are thus quite different phenomena. Families with husband unem-ployed have therefore been removed from the analysis. This removes the potential disturbing effect of husband's work status, rather than glossing over the problem (which is the typical strategy), and results can be generalized to the vast majority of families where the wife's choice of marketwork is a realistic family area of decision making. As stated earlier, it appears that the househusband role is not as yet a socially viable one in American culture. The operation of families in which the hus-band is unemployed requires separate analysis not possible here because of sample size. The elimination of non-job-holding husbands is not a theoretical choice in the sense that the *func-tionality* of the husband's participation in the labor force is assumed a priori (as the structural-functionalists once assumed that the wife's expressive housewife and mother role was the best functional alternative in industrial society). Rather, it is a methodological choice, in that the househusband role is not yet widely enough practiced to be treated as an option for most American families.

There are other reasons for excluding unemployed men from the analysis. As we have said, the low number of unemployed men ($N = 25$) in our sample makes independent analysis of this group difficult. Furthermore, there are definitional problems. The meaning of the term "unemployed" is very specific for census classifications (among other criteria, the respondent must be actively looking for work) but more vague in our survey, where the respondent (or his spouse) was simply offered "unemployed" as a category choice to classify husband's employment status. Indeed, less than half (12) of the male respondents who classified themselves as "unemployed" had actually received unemployment compensation in the past year. About 30 percent had received welfare payments. Thus, because of their low number, definitional problems, and the fact they constitute quite a different phenomenon than nonworking wives, they were deleted from the analysis.

In addition, all families with wives aged 65 and over were deleted from the sample, since only women *eligible* for an outside job should be included in a study of the allocation of both outside work and housework.

A FURTHER METHODOLOGICAL NOTE: ON SAMPLING WORKING WIVES

This analysis is cast in terms of the family, and many of the variables used are family variables. Yet only one person was interviewed (selected randomly) from each household, so that in about half the cases the husbands are respondents, and in the other half, wives. This introduces two potential kinds of problems: differences in perception, and sampling bias. Differences in perception are discussed later in the analysis. We turn now to the problem of sampling bias.

Comparison of the characteristics of our sample with census estimates for 1974 shows the two to be quite similar, except in one area. We found that the wives' labor force participation rate for employed husbands was close to the current population survey estimate for 1974 (46.8 in our sample versus 47.3 in the CPR estimate) for the male respondents. For female (wife) respondents, however, the comparable rate was substantially lower than it should have been (34.1 percent in our scale versus 47.3 percent in the CPR estimate). This underestimation for female respondents occurred in virtually all categories of the key predictor variables, and the size of the underestimation was unrelated to those variables. On reflection, it became clear that this undermeasurement of working wives among female respondents was not a fluke of our sample (nor a problem unique to this survey), but was likely to occur in any random sample. The review in the previous chapter of how time was spent pointed out that women's employment has a strong negative effect on time spent doing housework. Nevertheless, research has made it very clear that the working wife does much more *total* work than the nonworking wife or the working husband. It seemed obvious—post hoc—that working wives are less likely to be home for interviews than are housewives and, if home, much less likely to take the time—an hour and twenty minutes—to be interviewed. Since husbands seem to spend about the same amount of time on housework regardless of their wives' employment status, we find an accurate estimate of female labor force participation rates for male respondents.

A review of recent surveys turned up no discussion of this phenomenon, though there was no evidence that the problem was not present. Crude female labor force participation rates computed from Scanzoni (1970: 208, Table 2-2) show a 5 percent underestimation of female work rates for female respondents relative to male respondents. This survey was conducted in 1967 in Indianapolis. Since then, women's participation in the labor force has greatly increased, especially among heavy housework groups, such as wives with young children (Sweet, 1973; Hayghe, 1976). This might account for the somewhat larger gap in our data.

In the following analysis of female labor force participation, our focus will be on male respondents, since their sample of working wives seems quite accurate. In applying the same analysis to female respondents, it turned out that the predictor variable showed very similar patterns of relationships, but the total R^2 was a little lower. This fact, coupled with the fact that the underestimation for female respondents does not appear to be related to any of the predictor variables, makes it reasonable to assume that the error introduced by the underrepresentation of working wives among female respondents is random and only weakens the relationships, rather than changing their pattern or direction. In the analyses following this one, families with working and nonworking wives were studied separately, so that this underestimation phenomenon caused no problems and both male and female respondents could be studied. The following analysis using the female respondent sample is given in Appendix A, as are the multiple R^2s for the model using the two samples.

After the deletion from the sample of families with nonemployed men or wives aged 65 and over, the analysis was performed on the male respondent families. Wife's labor force participation was regressed on the five variables discussed earlier: husband's income, occupational prestige, education, wife's education, and stage in the family life cycle. The procedure used was a type of dummy variable regression analysis called Multiple Classification Analysis (Andrews et al., 1973). The advantage of dummy variable analysis is that all predictors can be put into categories, whether originally nominal, ordinal, or interval-level variables, and included together in the same analysis. Thus, variables such as family life-cycle stage can be entered into the same analysis with income or education. Since dummy variable analysis does not assume that the variables have linear effects, but only that there is no interaction, it is possible to discern the pattern of relationship for dependent and independent variables.

It will become obvious throughout the analysis of the data that some powerful predictors (such as education) show nonmonotonic patterns that would go unnoticed if the variables were entered as predictors measured at the interval level. It would be possible, of course, to approach the problem of nonlinearity by extensive analysis of scattergrams, tests of linearity, and the transformation of variables, but the dummy variable approach is more straightforward and easier to interpret. MCA is simply a form of dummy variable regression analysis in which coefficients are produced as deviations from the grand mean rather than the uncoded category mean. (It is an easy matter to go from one to the other with simple transformation formulas.) Dummy variable regression analysis (Bowen and Finegan, 1969), and MCA in particular (for example, Campbell et al., 1976), have grown in popularity in social science research in recent years. The results in the following analysis are presented both as adjusted and unadjusted category means, following common practice (see, for example, Bowen and Finegan, 1969).

Though the effects of husband's resources, wife's resources (here represented by her education), and family life-cycle stage are presented in two tables for practical reasons, the results are all drawn from a single MCA analysis in which the five variables are entered simultaneously to predict wife's labor force participation.

RESULTS

In Table 2.1, the adjusted and unadjusted effects of husband's resources are presented. First, a brief explanation of the notation: The adjusted wife's labor force participation rates are given for each category. Following each variable, a simple eta^2 and a measure of its adjusted effect, called $beta^2$, are presented (see Gove and Hughes, 1980, for a detailed explanation of $beta^2$). The beta statistic is useful as an indicator of the relative importance of that variable to the others in the analysis and in fact is directly analogous to eta except that the effects of the other independent variables have been adjusted for.[2] The significance of the variable is measured by an F-test based on a one-way analysis of variance model for both the adjusted and unadjusted sums of squares.

Table 2.1 shows the adjusted and unadjusted effects of husband's resources on wife's labor force participation. It is clear that husband's income shows the most powerful effect at the zero-order (unadjusted) level, and is approximately doubled in strength when adjusted for the other structural variables. Furthermore, a look at the adjusted means shows that when adjusted for the other variables in the model, the effect of husband's income on wife's work status is not smoothly linear but a kind of "step" function. The two categories "less than $4,999" and "5,000-8,999" have virtually identical labor force participation rates. Similarly, the 9,000-11,999 and 12,000-15,999 ranges show very similar rates. There is a sharp drop (about

TABLE 2.1   Effects of Husband's Resources on Wife's Labor
Force Participation (husband employed, wife's
age less than 65, male respondents)

| | Percentage of Wives Employed | | |
	Unadjusted	Adjusted[1]	(N)
Husband's Education			
Less than high school	37.6	38.2	(117)
High school	46.9	49.4	(143)
Some college	55.6	54.4	(72)
4 years of college	48.1	43.5	(77)
eta^2-beta^2	1.5	1.4	
Significance	NS	NS	
Husband's Income			
Less than $4,999	53.1	61.9	(32)
5,000– 8,999	58.0	62.0	(100)
9,000–11,999	47.8	47.2	(92)
12,000–15,999	43.9	42.1	(98)
16,000+	29.9	24.7	(87)
eta^2-beta^2	3.9	7.4	
Significance	$<.01$	$<.001$	
Husband's Occupational Status			
High	47.8	51.0	(67)
Medium	47.0	47.5	(215)
Low	43.0	40.7	(127)
eta^2-beta^2	.1	.6	
Significance	NS	NS	

1. Adjusted for wife's education, family life-cycle stage, and the other variables in
the table.

20 percent) above $16,000, however. The strong effect of husband's income is consistent with virtually every previous analysis of wife's labor force participation, including those based on census data.

Husband's occupational prestige shows the weakest effect of his "resource" variables. If one conceptualizes occupational prestige as a measure of the husband's "social productivity in marketwork," we would expect a lower rate of wife's participation in marketwork, the higher his occupational prestige. Though insignificant (at the .05 level), the effect is the opposite of that predicted.

There has been little research on the relationship of husband's occupational prestige to wife's work status. Using the 1/1000 census sample for 1960, Bowen and Fingean (1969: 154-158) found that occupational status (defined as occupational category or classification) does show a relationship of wife's labor force participation. Their women's labor force participation rates (adjusted for presence of children, wife's education, age, husband's employment status, other family income, and color) do show variation among occupational categories, ranging from a high of 41.3 for service workers to a low of 32.4 for professional-technical. But the "prestige" pattern is by no means monotonic; for example, "laborers" are second to professionals in wife's low work rates. They interpret these results as a *permanent income* effect—that is, occupational status is a better indicator of permanent income than current income, and permanent income as an independent effect on wife's predilection for work. However, it is clear that the results obtained from our sample show the effect of occupational prestige in and of itself to be quite weak.

If there is any effect of occupational prestige, it is the opposite of that which has been predicted, namely, the higher the husband's occupational status, the more likely the wife is to work. Though not explainable from a family resource perspective, an explanation for such a relationship is implicit in the structural-functionalist literature (see especially Parsons, 1949). From the literature, it can be argued that a similar location of husband and wife in the occupational prestige hierarchy can create disruption in a marital relationship. The stress on the marital relationship is manifest whenever the wife's occupational status substantially exceeds that of her husband.[3]

We know that wives are fairly concentrated in middle- and lower-status occupations, and that training and sex discrimination by and large limit them to such occupations (largely clerical and lower-status service occupations). As a consequence, the higher the husband's occupational prestige, the less threatened he will be and the less disrupted the marrige will be by the wife taking a typical job. Recent studies (Philliber and Hiller, 1978) indicate that the husband takes little status identification from his wife's occupational status, so that her taking a higher-status job than his offers him no positive prestige rewards. Thus, the independent effect of this occupational prestige (especially after controlling for his income) will be positive on wife's labor force participation. The pattern, however, is quite weak, and the above explanation should be taken primarily as a suggestion for further research.

The effect of husband's education falls between that of his income and occupational prestige. Though not quite achieving significance (at the .05 level) for male respondents, it does achieve significance (with the same pattern) for the total sample. Studies of wife's labor force participation (see, for example, Bowen and Finegan, 1969; Sweet, 1973) tend to ignore husband's education as a predictor. Just as wife's education is generally treated as a measure of earning potential (see, for example, Sweet, 1973: 51), husband's education may be thought of as a similar indicator and, when adjusted for his income as it is here, as a measure of long-term earning potential. Another interpretation is that education whets one's appetite for goods, in general leads to income expectations, and therefore an increased demand for money. Thus, ceteris peribus, the more highly educated the husband, the more he might encourage his wife to work. There is also an ideological interpretation of husband's education that makes a parallel prediction. This explanation holds that the more educated he is, the more likely he is to respect women's rights and not require that his wife occupy the traditional housewife role on ideological grounds. Either the appetite or ideology explanation might explain the increase in wife's labor force participation along with husband's education through the "some college" category. But the rather low level of wives' participation among families with husbands having completed college remains unexplained. Perhaps there is a more *efficient* use of income for the college educated (better saving and buying patterns). Perhaps college-educated husbands are more likely to be engaged in a career and to spend more time and energy at their jobs, leaving their wives with more responsibility for the household. This variable requires

TABLE 2.2 Effects of Wife's Education and Family Life-Cycle Stage on Wife's Labor Force Participation (husband employed, wife's age less than 65, male respondents)

	Percentage of Wives Employed		
	Unadjusted	*Adjusted*[1]	*(N)*
Wife's Education			
Less than high school	31.9	34.5	(97)
High school	49.7	46.8	(199)
Some college	42.5	47.4	(73)
4 years of college	67.5	66.9	(40)
$eta^2 - beta^2$	4.1	3.0	
Significance	<.001	<.01	
Family Life-Cycle Stage			
Prechild	78.0	63.3	(41)
Youngest Children at home:			
Less than 3 years	25.3	24.0	(87)
3– 5	40.0	39.0	(70)
6–11	48.4	52.8	(64)
12–18	62.0	63.7	(50)
Empty nest	42.7	47.2	(82)
Childless	60.0	63.7	(15)
$eta^2 - beta^2$	9.7	8.0	
Significance	<.001	<.001	

1. Adjusted for husband's education, income and occupational status, and for the other variables in the table.

more attention than it has received before a reliable explanation can be given.

Wife's education is a key variable in most models of wife's predilection for work. It increases the value of her market time more than the value of her housework time (except perhaps for child care; see Leibowitz, 1975). It also undoubtedly represents a selection effect, in that women who plan to work after marriage will pursue their education in order to find a better job. Table 2.2. shows this relationship. There is a great difference in working for high school dropouts (34.5 percent) and college graduates (66.9 percent), but there is virtually no difference between those who complete high school and those who also attend some college (46.8 and 47.4 percent, respectively). It seems probable that *some* college (no degree) is relatively worthless on the job market, particularly for women. Generally, a job either requires a college degree or can be done by anyone with a high school education; a few years of college make little difference. This pattern of labor force participation rates, then, suggests that the value-of-time effect may be more important than the selection explanation. But the value of time does not increase incrementally with years of schooling. Rather, the nature of the economic system creates a "step" effect. It might also be argued that the decision to leave college (or the inability to succeed there) may be an indication of a lack of interest in marketwork, a variation of a selection effect. Staying in college until one gets married and then leaving college may actually be a way to avoid working right after high school for some women, and this may balance off the slightly increased value of market time that a little college education produces.

Wife's education is used here as an indicator of her resources or relative potential productivity in the job and home areas. Other researchers have introduced a direct valuation of her wage rate in addition to her education, but this means of course that such a figure can only be estimated for nonworking women. Available estimation methods, such as income or occupational status of last job, can be criticized on the grounds that they are poor measures of the current value of her market time. The problems appear especially when earlier jobs were only part-time or supplementary and thus not indicative of present possibilities, given a desire for full-time work. Therefore, although wife's income and occupational prestige will be introduced later as predictors of housework allocation for working women, when looking at nonworking women and all women (both groups combined), education alone will be used as a measure of her potential market work productivity.

Definition of the family cycle is a more difficult task than it at first appears. Proper definition involves duration of marriage, presence of children, number of children, and ages of children. Age of husband and wife may also enter the criteria for placing families on some life-cycle continuum. As explained earlier, we focused on duration of marriage (less than or greater than seven years), presence of children, age of youngest child, and number of children.

Most studies based on 1960 census data show a clearly negative effect of number of children on wife's labor force participation and an equally sharp relationship between age of youngest child and labor force participation. In preliminary analyses of our 1973 survey data, the number of children had originally been combined with the age of youngest child in one overall "interaction" variable (this variable is used in Chapters 3 and 4). It became immediately obvious, however, that there was little change in wife's labor force participation rates as number of children increased, as long as age of youngest child was held constant. In analyses of both the male and female samples, it was found that this interaction variable yielded no increase in explained variance over a life-cycle variable that used only age of youngest child. In a separate regression analysis run only for families with children, age of youngest child and number of children were entered as separate variables, with the other structural variables as controls. The beta[2] for number of children was an insignificant 0.3. It was 7.9 percent for the age of youngest child variable. Thus, number of children adds no explanatory power to the model. For this reason it was deleted from the analysis of wife's work status. It will be of some importance, however, when the analysis shifts to desire for work (Chapter 3) and household division of labor (Chapter 4).

We used a variable, then, that focuses on age of youngest child as the primary determinant of family life-cycle stage. The results are shown in Table 2.2. Of all the variables in the structural model, this is the most powerful predictor of wife's labor force participation. Other researchers (Bowen and Finegan, 1969; Sweet, 1973) have shown that the age of the youngest child has a dramatic effect on decisions to enter the labor force.

Following the approach of Bowen and Finegan (1969), the stages of the family life cycle are defined in terms of the presence of children under 18 in the home and the age of the youngest child at home. Those couples who have had no children were divided into "prechild" and a much smaller "childless" category on the basis of their years of marriage (less than 7 versus 7 or more years). In this way, "synthetic" cohorts were created from cross-sectional data. As other researchers have pointed out (notably Sweet, 1973: 55-57), child status does not have a perfect one-to-one correlation with cohort time. Families can "jump backwards" as children age and a new child enters the family. Since we are primarily interested in the effects of a given household composition as a measure of "internal structure," however, such problems are not important here.

The presence of children introduces two kinds of effects: an increased need for money income and an increased demand for housework, including child care but definitely not limited to it. Available evidence, however, indicates that, as one might expect, the expenses of children increase with their age, while the demand for care and the impact on housework decrease as they get older. Therefore, one expects age of youngest child to be positively related to wife's labor force participation. All available evidence confirms this expectation.

This analysis confirms the strong effect of life-cycle stage on wife's work status. The adjusted labor force participation rate is only 24 percent when there are children under three years of age in the home, but 63.7 percent when the oldest children are teenagers. In fact, the teenage stage is quite comparable to the prechild stage (63.3 percent), when adjustments are made for the other structural variables. It is likely that the household demands of the teenage stage are more than offset by their financial requirements (and probably also by their help around the house). After children have left the home, however, there is a drop in wife's labor force participation, at least in part because the financial demands of children are substantially reduced, and because there is a reduced need for income on the basis of accumulated assets.

In general, the survey data yield results consistent with earlier studies and some new insights as well. For the wife's decision to work, it is the husband's wage rate, her potential wage rate, and the demand for child care that primarily determine the choice of outside work role allocation for the family. The economic model works well, as expected, except for the surprising finding that the number of children has little effect. Yet we see also that characteristics of the socioeconomic system in which the family finds itself affect the family in sometimes unexpected ways. Wife's education does not affect the family in a linear fashion but as a step function, since the society in some ways values certificates of education more than it does education itself.

The family's choice of a work allocation system, then, appears to be partly explainable in terms of rational adaptation to objective circumstances. Yet the sociological focus on attitudes and role expectations, best exemplified in the role theorists' approach to the family (for example, see Nye, 1976), deserves a direct comparison with the predictive power of more objective variables. For that reason, we turn to the analysis of sex-role ideology of husbands and wives and its effect on their choice of a work allocation system.

SEX-ROLE IDEOLOGY: TWO SCALES

The sex-role ideology of husbands and wives is generally ignored by economists in their models of family role structure or, if not totally ignored, included under a general term like "tastes," or in an error term. Sociologists have been explicitly concerned with the issue for quite a while, and an endless number of college surveys exist to support various theories about the socialization and family background determinants of sex-role ideology and the effects that such an ideology has on the need for achievement. Rarely, however, is the ideology of married couples measured against behavior in terms of household task allocation (see Chapter 1 for a summary of the few that do). It is clearly an important factor in the allocation of roles, however, and should be studied relative to other, "harder" predictors of behavior based on economic models.

To elicit feelings toward proper sex roles in society and in the family, respondents were given a list of 24 items covering a range of sex-role-related attitudes, from rather strongly liberal, pro-feminist attitudes ("a housewife should be paid a salary for the work she does") to typical traditional-ideology items ("a

woman's place is in the home"). Both male and female respondents were handed a printed list of the lettered items and
asked to indicate by letter which statements they agreed with. It
was felt that by not being forced to express agreement or disagreement with the items, and by being allowed simply to indicate the items by letters, the respondent was not pressured to
make a decision on items of which he or she was unsure or
actually had no opinion, and that only items he or she definitely
agreed with would be indicated.

The responses for the entire sample (unmarried statuses as
well as married) were factor analyzed using a principal components solution, and the factors were rotated using a variety of
methods. Two factors, of five and eight items, consistently
emerged in these analyses. The items are presented in Table
2.3.

The distinction between the two scales is immediately obvious.
The first, labeled the "Traditional Sex-Role Ideology Scale,"
is made up entirely of items endorsing the traditional view of
male and female roles. There is a fairly wide range in the extent
to which respondents agreed to the different items (a range of
11.8 percent to 63.6 percent for females). For particular items,
the proportion of married men and women who agreed was
roughly similar, although men in 4 out of the 5 cases were more
likely to endorse items reflecting the traditional view. In general,
these five items represent an adequate summary of the traditional
role prescriptions for men and women. It is thus clear that a
high score on this scale is a positive endorsement of traditional
sex roles rather than of sterotypes about men and women. They
are beliefs about "proper" behavior.

The second scale, also presented in Table 2.3, is labeled the
"Women's Independence Ideology Scale." Just as with the list
for the previous scale, many of the items concern proper behavior,
except that each of these items is an endorsement of women's
rights. It is no accident that the statement, "I agree with the
goals of the Women's Liberation Movement," falls solidly into
this cluster. Again, there is a wide range in the proportion of respondents endorsing particular items, but as with the other
scale, the proportion of men and women who agree with par-

TABLE 2.3 Sex-Role Ideology Scales (married sample)

	Percentage Agreeing	
	Male	Female
Traditional Sex-Role Ideology Scale		
(1) When couples are dating, the man should always be the one to ask for the date.	58.1	63.6
(2) The man should always be the one to suggest sex.	13.8	11.8
(3) Girls should be trained to be homemakers, and boys for an occupation suited to their talents.	36.8	29.1
(4) Motherhood is the ideal "career" for most women.	41.9	34.2
(5) I think a woman's place is in the home.	38.5	27.2
Women's Independence Ideology Scale		
(1) I agree with the goals of the Women's Liberation Movement.	27.3	24.9
(2) A woman should have as much independence as a man.	67.9	65.3
(3) The wife should have as much say as the husband on decisions like buying a car.	79.0	79.9
(4) A woman should be free to have an abortion if she chooses.	43.7	47.7
(5) A woman should be eligible for any job regardless of her sex.	62.0	73.6
(6) A housewife should be paid a salary for the housework she does.	10.1	13.6
(7) A husband should regularly help his wife with the housework.	58.4	44.2
(8) A woman can pursue a full-time career and be a good mother.	44.6	58.6

ticular items was remarkably similar. In fact, more men than women expressed agreement with three of the Women's Independence items, and men and women responded in virtually the same way in another.

Hesselbart (1976) also found two factors in her analysis of 27 items. She labeled them "Pro-Women's Equality" and "Anti-Women's Equality." An examination of the items in her scales indicates that three out of the five of her pro-equality items concern the legal rights of women; one asks for approval of the Women's Liberation Movement, and one concerns the existence of sex discrimination. Her anti-equality scale is a mixture of negative role prescriptions ("Women with pre-school children should *not* work if at all possible") and sex stereotypes ("Women have trouble making decisions"). Her two scales are weakly related ($R = -.20$ for women and $-.11$ for men). These weak interrelationships indicate that these scales really do measure two different attitude clusters. It thus appears that a woman, for example, can agree that the best role for women is that of housewife and mother and even prefer the traditional courtship procedures, yet at the same time demand independence from and equality with her husband and other men *within* those sex roles.

These two lists of items were summed and the resulting distributions of totals collapsed into two categories of approximately equal size. These two dichotomized scales were then entered into a dummy variable regression analysis along with the "structural" items treated earlier—husband's income, education, and occupation; life-cycle stage; and wife's education.[4] The results are presented in Table 2.4. Since only the respondent's sex-role ideology was measured, the results are presented separately for husbands and wives. All relationships are in the predicted direction—that is, the less traditional the ideology of both husband and wife, the more likely the wife is to work, adjusting for the structural variables.

The adjusted effects are statistically significant ($p < .001$) only for the wife's endorsement of the traditional sex-role ideology. Neither scale predicts wife's work status significantly (at the .05 level), though the Women's Independence Scale does show a weak but significant effect ($eta^2 = 1.9$ percent) before controls. Traditional sex-role attitudes show no effect before or after controls.

For wives, the significant effect of traditional sex-role attitudes is actually increased slightly by the structural controls. The effect of nonsignificant Women's Independence attitudes is a bit stronger before controls, but it is still not significant at the .05 level.

TABLE 2.4   Effects of Sex-Role Ideology on Wife's Labor Force
Participation (husband employed, wife's age less than 65)

| | Percentage of Women Working | | | | | |
| | Husband's Ideology[1] | | | Wife's Ideology[2] | | |
	Unadj.	Adj.[3]	(N)	Unadj.	Adj.[3]	(N)
Sex-Role Ideology						
Nontraditional	50.5	48.7	(210)	42.0	42.7	(257)
Traditional	41.2	43.1	(199)	24.1	23.2	(195)
eta^2-beta^2	0.9	0.3		3.4	4.2	
Significance	NS	NS		1t<.001	1t<.001	
Women's Independence Ideology						
Nontraditional	54.1	50.4	(170)	37.4	35.4	(203)
Traditional	40.2	42.8	(239)	31.7	33.4	(249)
eta^2-beta^2	1.9	0.6		0.4	0.1	
Significance	NS	NS		NS	NS	

1. Male respondents.
2. Female respondents.
3. Adjusted for husband's education, income, and occupational status; wife's education; family life-cycle stage; and the other ideology variable in the table.

Taking the two scales together, the total r^2 for husband's ideology is only 1.9 percent, of which 1.1 percent is actually not independent of the structural model. Wife's ideology, on the other hand, showed a total effect of 3.1 percent on labor force participation, and virtually all of the explanatory power of their ideology is independent of the structural model. Furthermore, if the female respondent sample contains more random error, as was suggested earlier, then this 3.1 percent is probably an underestimate of the effect of her ideology on her choice of outside work. It is clear that it is the wife's ideology rather than that of her husband that affects the wife's decision to work. And it is her lack of adherence to the traditional sex role prescriptions, rather than her positive support of women's rights, that most affects her behavior. Nevertheless, it seems clear that the woman's choice of work status is not simply a product of her attitude toward proper sex roles, but a response to her family's social and economic needs as well.

The use of attitudinal variables in cross-sectional surveys inevitably raises the problem of causal direction. It might be argued, for example, that a woman's ideology arises from her experience as worker or housewife. One study (Molm, 1978) presents data suggesting that this might be the case. Thus the effect of her experience shows itself in her attitudes, but not those of her husband. With the present data, no meaningful resolution of this problem can be reached. The ramifications of these results concerning sex-role ideology are examined more fully in Chapter 6.

Appendix A
Factors Affecting Wife's Labor Force Participation: Female
Respondents (husband employed, wife's age less than 65)

	Percentage of Wives Employed		
	Unadjusted	*Adjusted*	*(N)*
Husband's Education			
Less than high school	25.4	22.2	(114)
High school	38.8	40.9	(160)
Some college	41.0	41.3	(78)
4 years of college	32.1	30.1	(100)
eta^2-beta^2	1.6	2.8	
Significance	NS	.01	
Husband's Income			
Less than $4,999	59.5	63.8	(42)
5,000- 8,999	29.7	32.3	(91)
9,000-11,999	35.3	34.1	(116)
12,000-15,999	38.7	38.9	(111)
16,000+	20.7	17.3	(92)
eta^2-beta^2	4.7	6.5	
Significance	.001	.001	
Husband's Occupational Status			
High	29.9	30.7	(117)
Medium	36.6	35.4	(243)
Low	33.7	35.9	(92)
eta^2-beta^2	0.4	0.2	
Significance	NS	NS	
Wife's Education			
Less than high school	29.9	26.1	(117)
High school	33.8	33.5	(195)
Some college	32.1	33.8	(81)
4 years of college	47.5	54.1	(59)
eta^2-beta^2	1.3	3.0	
Significance	NS	.001	

(continued)

APPENDIX A (Continued)

	Percentage of Wives Employed		
	Unadjusted	*Adjusted*	*(N)*
Family Life-Cycle Stage			
Prechild	47.2	35.7	(36)
Youngest:			
Less than 3 years	19.0	16.2	(100)
3– 5	28.0	28.0	(93)
6–11	39.3	43.3	(89)
12–18	46.3	47.7	(54)
Empty nest	40.0	42.5	(70)
Childless	50.0	58.7	(10)
eta^2-beta^2	4.7	6.3	
Significance	.01	.001	

	Respondents	
	Male	*Female*
R^2 Structural Variables	18.5	14.8
R^2 Ideological Variables	1.9	3.1
R^2 All Variables	19.3	18.6

NOTES

1. Some researchers, notably Bowen and Finegan (1969), have run separate analyses by race when using census samples. Because of the smaller sample size here, such a breakdown was not possible. The variable could not be used as a predictor variable because of certain expected interaction effects.

2. The formula for $beta^2$ is Di/T, where Di is the sum of squares based on the deviations for predictor i adjusted for the other predictors. Eta^2, of course, is simply the explained sum of squares (unadjusted) divided by the total sum of squares.

3. This entire question is addressed in detail by Oppenheimer (1977). She derives from Parson's writing suggestions of both a "status maintenance" effect—wherein status consistency is viewed positively—and of the "status competition" effect proposed here. She proposes some evidence that the status consistence effect is predominant, but does not specifically measure occupational prestige, nor does she control for other variables. Her only analysis of wife's labor force participation is based on a sample of recently employed wives. Therefore, her results are not clearly interpretable.

4. These ideology variables are not entered as controls to determine the independent effects of the structural variables because it is not clear what the causal direction is for the ideology variables (see, for example, Molm, 1978). If the primary direction of effect is from work status to attitudes, controlling for the attitude variables will yield invalid estimates of the independent effects of the structural variables.

3

Wife's Work and the Desire to Work

The previous chapter focused on the determinants of the role actually chosen by wives—the causes for their entry into the labor force or their decision to stay at home. As pointed out in the introductory chapter, though one can explain a wife's choice between worker and housewife roles as a semi-rational adjustment to circumstances, any decision involves costs as well as benefits. For example, though a working mother brings in income that raises the standard of living for her family, or brings her self-satisfaction, she must perform more total work (see Chapter 4) and might worry about whether or not her children are getting proper care.

Measurements of behavior speak to the question of profit, of ultimate choices, of the outcome of a calculation of costs and rewards. Some choices are easier than others, since some, though necessary (that is, rational), involve higher costs than others. Some choices are experienced as more forced or constrained than others. This chapter will focus on the determinants of labor force participation from a somewhat different perspective than that of the previous chapter. The central question asked is: "Given the decision to work or not to work outside the home, what is the nature of that choice? Is it experienced as forced—that is, as contrary to the preferences of husband or wife? What are the key variables that determine this 'forcedness'?" Put another way, this analysis measures the role preferences of women who have already chosen a role; if the wife works, the analysis asks if she *wants* to work or if she feels *compelled* to work despite her desire or her husband's preferences.

It asks if the housewife wants to work—that is, if she feels compelled to stay home despite her desires. The analysis seeks those characteristics of the wife, her husband, and her family that determine these conditions. This notion of the "forcedness" of the married woman's role is a central feature of recent women's liberation literature. Both research literature and more popular books movies, and television depictions of the woman's role emphasize the fulfilling nature of the outside job and the sense of trapped loneliness and stagnancy experienced by the housewife. The assumption is that the woman is held in the housewife role by either (1) the demands of that role—particularly the desires of her husband and the needs of her children, or (2) the lack of her opportunity in the job market—a function either of the market itself, her own lack of preparation, or both. This literature implies that the demands of husband and family run contrary to the woman's own desires, and that as a result, she must stay home. In general she feels forced or trapped into any situation that does not contribute to her personal fulfillment, which comes largely from outside employment.

A less ideological view of this "forcedness" would describe the desire to occupy a role one does not occupy as residual pressure not (or not yet) expressed in behavior. If movement between roles is preceded by a desire to change roles, and since work-role change typically involves time, costs, and reorganization—sometimes massive—of other life roles, discordance between role desire and role occupancy may simply signify the likelihood of future movement rather than enslavement in the housewife or worker role.

To study the fulfillment of desire rather than just behavior requires a discussion of motivation (the focus of desire) and the mesh between motive and relevant conditions (the possibilities for fulfillment). A preliminary theory thus requires a statement of the motives wives typically give for working or wanting to work, as well as a discussion of which characteristics of the wife and her family are most salient to the fulfillment of those motivations and how those characteristics should be related to that fulfillment.

The best studies of motivation appear in work commitment research. Though the present analysis is not viewed as a study of work commitment, there is enough similarity between the desire to work and work commitment to make the research in the latter area relevant. Serious empirical research in the area may be dated from Sobol's (1973) study of a 1955 national sample. This study and that of Fogarty et al. (1971) defined work commitment as future work plans. It has been defined differently in more recent studies. For example, Haller and Rosenmayer (1971) distinguish between work plans and work wishes. Sobol (1973) extended the work commitment concept to include a scale of depth of commitment, including both behavior and plans. Safilios-Rothschild (1970) defined work commitment as the investment of time, interest, energy, and emotion in work relative to other areas of life. The present analysis is concerned with an investigation of the overall preference for a wife to work outside the home, both that of the wife and that of her husband. Though this approach is somewhat different from that of those interested in work commitment, a review of the findings of this literature will be useful.

In general, findings related to future work plans are similar to those of labor force participation studies: wife's work commitment decreases with husband's income and increases with wife's income and education. It decreases with the presence of children and increases with past work involvement. Of more immediate importance here is the study of the motivations behind the decision to work and the relationship between motivation and behavior.

In general, researchers agree that financial reasons are by far the most frequently expressed motivations for work among working women (Sobol, 1973; Rosenfeld and Perrella, 1965). Better-educated women, women with no children, and women whose husbands have higher incomes are more likely to give reasons related to personal satisfaction. Financial reasons are thus predominant, but they are not as closely related to work commitment as other motivations, though the differences in strength of relationship tend to be small. Sobol (1974) found that, in descending order of strength, the need to accomplish, the need to occupy time, participation in a family business, and chronic and temporary financial problems were all related to future work plans among working women. (The motivation analysis was not run for housewives.) This result might be misleading in terms of our present interest in the desire for work, because it might be expected that future work plans might not be strongly related to financial need if the respondent expects improvement in his or her financial condition. Haller and Rosenmayer (1971), however, found that nonfinancial motivation also showed a strong connection with *wishes* for a long-term employment, as well as plans for work. It seems obvious, almost tautological, that women who work for personal satisfaction are more likely to prefer working (now or in the future) than women who work for financial reasons only, since one's financial situation can be quite fluid, and it may be common to be optimistic about one's financial future.

Motivations are often included as just one of many influences on the wife's decision to work. Researchers classify the kinds of factors influencing work plans in various ways. Sobol divided the factors into (1) enabling conditions—family status variables, including pregnancy and future child expectations; (2) facilitating conditions—wife's education and previous work experience; and (3) precipitating conditions—financial factors, including husband and wife's income, and attitudinal factors, such as life satisfaction, need for accomplishment, or occupation of time. Morgan et al. (1966) suggest the terms "constraints," "pressures," and "more discretionary motives," roughly paralleling Sobol's three groups. Since this analysis is specifically concerned with the "forcedness" of a role position (either of working wife or housewife), we are interested in classifying the variety of factors influencing work in terms of their possible contribution to forcing a woman to occupy either the workers or housewife role against her preferences or those of her husband. The concept of forcedness is relative, of course. It implies here only that the woman, given her personal preference, would not be in the position she is in. She acts contrary to her preferences, it is proposed, for two related reasons. One is the decision to maximize her family's immediate utility instead of her own. As we have seen, this fits in well with economists' treatment of the family as a utility-maximizing unit. The women's liberation literature also sees this as a prime source of dissatisfaction. The second reason is the existence of conditions that prevent the attainment of desires. For example, a woman may desire an exciting, well-paying, high-prestige job, but if she is poorly educated, she is unable to attain that goal. She cannot simply "choose" that kind of job.

The first factor, the desire to maximize family utility over one's own, should be closely related to those "enabling" conditions listed by Sobol, particularly family composition. Though most studies find no detrimental effect of mother's employment on children (see, for example, the review by Hoffman, 1974) there is still a strong belief by women that their employment can have a negative effect on their children. Of our female sample, 56 percent disagreed with the statement that "a woman can pursue a full-time career and be a good mother" (see Table 3, Chapter 2). Their husbands expressed similar feelings. The desires of her husband are important in the wife's decision to work, and some wives may try to satisfy their spouse rather than themselves. In general, then, we might describe the effect of the ages and number of children as an indicator of choice of work relating to family utility maximization. This relationship refers both to the decision to work as well as the decision to stay home. Number of children is postively related to the family's need for home goods as well as market goods. Thus we might expect that, ceteris paribus, working women worry about the home goods they are not providing, and housewives worry about money they could be making. Either way, there should be an increased sensation of "constrainedness" with an increasing number of children. In addition, age of youngest child should be related to the desire to stay home. Housewives may feel trapped in the home with younger children present. Older children create more monetary strain but may also trap the wife in the housewife role.

From the economists' point of view, a woman's decision to enter marketwork is partly contingent both on her husband's wage rate and on her potential wage rate. But for a variety of reasons—ideology and "tastes" among them—a woman may violate the dictates of pure economic rationality. Despite her husband's low income, for example, she may choose not to work because of personal tastes or household circumstances, yet still feel that she is letting her family down. Or she may work despite a lack of family need, for reasons of personal satisfaction. On the other hand, the wife may work because the family needs the money, although she prefers not to. Here, maximization of the family's utility over her own immediate satisfaction causes her to act against her general preferences, or those of her husband. For the same reasons, her own income or her potential income (as measured by her education) may cause her to work despite her desires because the family needs the money. Her education, besides being a proxy for potential income, may also be related to a more liberal ideology, or it may reflect a selection effect, wherein the wife has pursued a higher education precisely because she wants to have a career.

Thus, the effects of husband's income and education and those of his wife are likely to be complex. It is expected that the same variables that predict women's labor force participation—income and education of husband and wife, family composition, and sex-role ideology—would also predict experienced "forcedness" of the occupation of worker or housewife role. Other sociological variables, such as the occupational prestige of husband and wife (if she works), should have some effect. Whether or not the wife works full or part time is also expected to matter. In general, then, this analysis parallels in many respects the model of wife's labor force participation outlined in the previous chapter. Since the housewife and wife-working families must be treated separately in order to properly measure discordance between preferred and occupied roles, other variables can be included for the working wife that are not included in the analysis of labor force participation rates. Specifically, her income, occupational prestige, and part-time/full-time status are added to the model. Our attention will now turn to measurement of the dependent preference variables themselves.

MEASURES OF PREFERENCE

Past studies of marital role satisfaction have determined that the freedom of choice one has in the occupation of roles is an important determinant of personal and marital satisfaction (see Chapter 5). Therefore, the questionnaire was designed to include measures of desire for the work role both among housekeepers and among working wives.

Housewives—those married women who were not employed at the time of the interview—were asked: "Do you wish you had a job now? (Yes/No)." If the wife was employed, she was asked to agree or disagree with the statement: "If I had my choice, I would rather not be working." Thus, both housewives and working wives were able to express their sentiments toward the role of outside workers and to do so in terms of their present situation.

In addition to the wife's preference for a work or housewife role, that of the husband was also obtained, though not from him. As explained in Chapter 2, wives were asked their husband's preferences, but husbands were asked neither their own preferences for their wife's employment status nor their wife's preferences. Therefore, only the female respondents (wives) could be used for analysis. They were asked: Would your husband prefer that you worked or did not work? Thus we have only the wife's perception of her husband's preference. This in itself, however, is an important consideration for the wife's perception of her husband's feelings toward her choice of roles, and is probably more important in her choice than the husband's actual feelings. This variable was dichotomized (0 = did not work, 1 = worked), and its mean is simply the percentage of wives in some category who perceived their husbands as preferring them to work outside the home. The wife's desire to work was similarly coded.

The wife's and the husband's preference variables will be treated primarily as dependent variables in the following analysis, since we are interested in the impact of both structural and ideological variables on the concordance between the desire for work and occupation of the work role. First, though, it will be instructive to investigate the impact of the wife's and her husband's perceived desire on her choice of work role, relative to both the structural and ideological variables and to each other. To that end, the wife's desire for work and that of her husband (as perceived by her) were added to the models outlined in the previous chapter as predictors of her actual labor force participation.

Table 3.1 presents the results in three ways. First, the unadjusted effect of wife's desire and husband's perceived desire for the working wife role on the wife's labor force participation is given. As might be expected, the effect is powerful. The wife's preference explains 27.2 percent of her behavior, while the husband's perceived preference accounts for 19.7 percent. Nevertheless, 10.5 percent of wives who do not wish to do in fact work outside the home, and 40.1 percent of those who wish to work do not. In addition, 20.1 percent of wives work against their husband's perceived preference, and 35.6 percent do not work, even though they think their husbands want them to. Here we see clear evidence of the pressure on women to take an outside job, both as a result of their own desires and those of their husbands.

When the two measures of preference are entered into a regression equation with the structural predictors of wife's labor force participation (see Chapter 2), the effect of the preference variables is reduced somewhat, though it is still strong. The correlation between preference and behavior, then, is partly a reflection of structural conditions and partly of other, probably more personal, factors. The addition of the wife's sex-role ideology as a control makes little difference, however, indicating that these other factors are not ideological.

To investigate more fully the effect of the wife's preference relative to that of her husband (as she perceives it), the interaction of the two in their prediction of wife's labor force participation was investigated. Table 3.2 presents the effect of wife's preference on her actual role within categories of her husband's perceived preference, and vice versa. When husband and wife disagree (33.8 percent of the sample), the wife's preference is

TABLE 3.1 Effects of Wife's Preference and Husband's Perceived Preference on Wife's Labor Force Participation (husband employed, female respondents, wife's age less than 65)

	Unadjusted	Adj. for Structural Variables	Adj. for Structural Variables & Wife's Ideology	(N)
Wife's Preference				
No work	10.5	15.7	16.4	(228)
Work	59.9	53.9	53.1	(197)
$eta^2 - beta^2 - beta^2$	27.2	16.3	15.0	(425)
Significance	.001	.001	.001	
Husband's Perceived Preference				
No work	20.1	25.1	25.3	(303)
Work	66.4	54.0	53.5	(122)
$eta^2 - beta^2 - beta^2$	19.7	7.7	7.3	(425)
Significance	.001	.001	.001	

more likely to win out. Given her preference, however, the husband's perceived agreement or disagreement still has a strong impact on her behavior. For example, if she wants to work and she thinks her husband prefers otherwise, she works in 45 percent of the cases. If her husband is perceived to agree, this figure rises to 77 percent.

"Forcedness" (or, less ideologically, role change pressure) is clearly present. A full 25 percent of wives do not occupy the role they prefer. Their actual roles violate the perceived preferences of their husbands in 24 percent of the cases, yet they often do not agree with their husbands. The wife's actual role violates either her own preference or that of her husband 41 percent of the time.

To analyze the nature of this discordance is to study the tension created by conflicting demands. Whenever two or more individuals seek to minimize the utility of the group, and to do so under imperfect social and economic conditions, something must be compromised, and in most societies, it is the wife's

TABLE 3.2   Interaction of Wife's Preference and Husband's Perceived
Preference on Wife's Labor Force Participation

	Percentage of Wives Working					
Husband's			*Wife's Preference*			
Perceived Preference	*No Work*		*Work*		*Total[1]*	
No work	7	(214)	45	(116)	20	(330)
Work	39	(36)	77	(93)	66	(129)
Total[1]	12	(250)	59	(209)	33	(459)

1. Total percentages do not exactly equal those in Table 3.1 because of missing
values in the control variables removed both from the unadjusted and adjusted means.

choice of role that is most vulnerable to such pressures. We
now turn to a study of the loci of this tension or forcedness in the
allocation of work roles among family members, specifically
aimed at the wife's role. It is assumed that the same variables
that influence the actual choice of wife's work role will also
affect the discord within, or the forcedness of, her occupation
of that role.

We proceed with the analysis by studying the determinants
of the desire to work within housewife and within working-wife
families. Table 3.3 presents the baseline figures for the desire
to work among these two types of families. The husband is perceived to be less likely to want the wife to work, whether the
wife actually works or not.

More than one-quarter of the housewives want to work outside the home, while 17.8 percent of the working wives want to
be full-time housewives. Thus, pressure tends to be in the direction of the working-wife role. As the wife defines the husband's
point of view, pressure is in the opposite direction: 42.9 percent
of the husbands of working wives would rather their wives did
not work, while only 14.1 percent of housewives' husbands
want them to work.

As in the previous chapter, the effects of husband's resources,
wife's resources, family life-cycle stage, and sex-role ideology
will be presented and discussed separately, but the adjusted
values of the predicted variables (wife's desire for work and
husband's perceived preference) are generated in a single regression analysis. Specifically, the husband's resource variables,

TABLE 3.3   Percentage of Wives Who Prefer to Work and Who
Perceive Their Husbands as Preferring Them to Work
(female respondents, husband employed)

		(N)
Housewives:		
Wife prefers to work	26.7	(295)
Husband prefers wife to work	14.1	(295)
Working Wives:		
Wife prefers to work	82.2	(140)
Husband prefers wife to work	57.1	(140)

the wife's resource variables, and the family life-cycle variable
are entered simultaneously in a single regression run using the
MCA procedure described in the previous chapter. These runs
are done here separately for housewives and working wives,
and as we shall see, this allows us to expand the number of
wife's resource variables. Finally, to obtain the adjusted values
of the sex-role ideology variable, the regression analyses are
rerun with these variables added to the model.

HUSBAND'S RESOURCES

We turn first to the effect of the husband's linkages to the
socioeconomic system. The analysis of labor force participation in the previous chapter found husband's income to be a
relatively strong negative predictor of wife's labor force participation, husband's education to have a weak and unclear
effect, and occupational prestige to have a weak but positive
effect. Once the choice has been made, however, we may ask
whether the desire to work shows the same patterns. For example, does the housewife want to work more the lower her husband's income, or vice versa? Table 3.4 gives the unadjusted
and adjusted percentages of the wives and husbands who want
the wife to work as the precentages are predicted by the husband's resource variables.

Among the housewives, none of the husband's resource variables is a significant predictor of the wife's desire for work or
her perception of her husband's preference, and even the general
patterns are sometimes unclear. Both husband's income and
education are significant predictors of wife's preference when

TABLE 3.4   Effects of Husband's Resources on Husband's
and Wife's Preferences for Wife's Outside Job
(husband employed, female respondents)

| | *Percentage Desiring Wife to Work* | | | | |
| | *Wife's Preference* | | | *Husband's Preference* | |
Housewives (295)	*Unadj.*	*Adj.*	*(N)*	*Unadj.*	*Adj.*
Husband's Education					
Less than high school	27.2	26.5	(88)	7.8	10.1
High school	37.1	34.7	(97)	17.3	18.3
Some college	13.6	14.7	(44)	9.1	9.1
4 years of college	19.7	23.5	(66)	21.2	16.6
eta^2-beta^2	3.6	2.3		2.5	1.3
Significance	.05	NS		NS	NS
Husband's Income					
Less than $4,999	25.0	20.4	(20)	15.0	17.7
5,000– 8,999	39.1	34.9	(64)	20.0	19.6
9,000–11,999	29.3	28.6	(75)	10.7	10.9
12,000–15,999	15.4	16.9	(65)	7.5	7.5
16,000+	23.9	28.4	(17)	18.3	17.7
eta^2-beta^2	3.3	2.1		2.0	1.9
Significance	.05	NS		NS	NS
Husband's Occupational Status					
High	18.5	21.7	(81)	18.5	13.6
Medium	28.0	28.1	(150)	12.4	14.7
Low	34.4	30.0	(64)	12.5	13.2
eta^2-beta^2	1.6	0.5		0.6	0.0
Significance	NS	NS		NS	NS
Working Wives (140)					
Husband's Education					
Less than high school	69.0	80.1	(29)	37.9	43.8
High school	81.4	82.4	(59)	59.3	66.4
Some college	81.5	80.2	(27)	70.4	59.2
4 years of college	100.0	85.9	(25)	64.0	52.5
eta^2-beta^2	6.4	0.3		4.9	3.2
Significance	.05	NS		NS	NS

TABLE 3.4 (Continued)

| Working Wives (140) | Percentage Desiring Wife to Work | | | | | |
| | Wife's Preference | | | Husband's Preference | |
	Unadj.	Adj.	(N)	Unadj.	Adj.
Husband's Income					
Less than $4,999	76.2	83.5	(21)	66.7	67.4
5,000– 8,999	82.1	88.3	(28)	60.7	53.6
9,000–11,999	76.3	78.9	(38)	60.5	64.6
12,000–15,999	84.2	78.1	(38)	44.7	42.7
16,000+	100.0	87.2	(15)	66.7	74.0
eta^2–beta^2	3.4	1.2		2.9	4.9
Significance	NS	NS		NS	NS
Husband's Occupational Status					
High	100.0	93.5	(30)	66.7	70.3
Medium	83.0	83.2	(81)	54.3	53.7
Low	62.0	67.5	(29)	58.6	56.5
eta^2–beta^2	10.4	4.9		1.0	1.8
Significance	.001	.05		NS	NS

not adjusted for the other variables in the model, but their effect is weakened with controls. Housewives whose husbands have a high school education or less are more likely to want an outside job than do those with more educated husbands. The effect of husband's income is nonmonotonic, generally negative in the unadjusted cases but becoming indeterminate with controls.

Husband's education has a weakly positive impact on role satisfaction among housewives. If his education is primarily a measure of future or potential income, then a family utility explanation suffices, since it means that housewives whose husbands are poorly educated can only obtain a better standard of living by going to work in the outside world. If husband's education is negatively related to the traditionality of his sex-role ideology, then the wives of less educated husbands are trapped by their husband's view of their proper role. But the husband's perceived preference (see Table 3.4) shows no consistent relationship to his education. Thus, the family utility explanation is better supported by the evidence.

The weak independent effect of the husband's income, both on his wife's and his own preference for her to have an outside job, is hard to explain. One possible explanation is that two different, contradictory effects are present. One, the wife feels more of a duty to work, the lower her husband's income. In opposition to this effect, there is less need to work when husband's income is high, so that she will not work even if desired to do so. Thus, at lower income levels, desire to work is an expression of the desire to maximize the family's utility (and her own lifestyle), whereas at higher income levels, the desire to work is a quest for the personal satisfaction that can be derived from an outside job.

Husband's occupational status has a weak but clearly negative effect on wife's desire to work, though virtually no effect on his own perceived perference. Again, this may be a type of potential income effect, where the wife can expect no improvement in her family's standard of living unless she goes to work. Upward mobility is rarer at low occupational status levels, just as it is at lower educational levels. This may also be the result of an effect discussed in the previous chapter. There we found that wives were less likely to work, the lower the husband's occupational status level. One explanation proposed was that her working would be more of a threat to his status, the lower that status was. Perhaps the larger number of dissatisfied women when the husband's occupational status level is low is a result of more of these women choosing not to work, even though they would prefer it. In addition, they may be "forced" into the housewife role by the more traditional sex-role ideology of both the husband and wife at lower occupational levels. Among working wives, the effect of the husband's resource variables on preference for work is somewhat stronger than it is among housewives. Occupational prestige in particular is a strong positive predictor of the working wife's preference for the role she occupies, just as it is for housewives. In addition, the husband's perceived preference parallels that of the wife, though the effect is rather weak.

The effects of the husband's education and income are similar: positive on her preference for work without controls, but virtually nonexistent with controls. Since the strength of each variable in the model tends to decrease after controls except family life-cycle stage, it appears that the tendency of families with poorly educated and low-income husbands to have larger numbers of children may account for the decreased satisfaction of the working wife at lower income and educational levels.

Overall, the husband's resource variables are rather weak predictors of husband's and wife's preferences for the wife to work, except in the case of husband's occupational status among working wives. This is best explained by status conflict between working spouses, rather than an emphasis on maximizing the family's economic utility.

WIFE'S RESOURCES

Study of the effect of the wife's resource variables reveals an interesting pattern. Those measures of the wife's resources more related to her personal satisfaction have more impact on her pattern of preferences, while those more reflective of family utility tend to have more impact on her perception of her husband's preference.

Looking first at the relationships for working wives, it is clear that her educational level and to a much lesser extent, her occupational status, have a positive effect on her job commitment. These variables are important in the personal satisfaction the wife obtains from her job and may also reflect her motivation to obtain work in the first place (see Table 3.5).

The wife's income and her part- or full-time status may be more reflective of family utility than of her personal satisfaction. These show up as having a strong impact on her perception of her husband's preference, but not on her own preference for the worker role.

As we pointed out earlier, the effect of a wife's education on the satisfaction she derives from the housewife role is difficult to predict, though we know it makes a difference once she has taken a job. For housewives, then, the effect of wife's education on her desire to work is unclear and, as we see, this is precisely the way it appears empirically. The husbands, however, re-

TABLE 3.5   Effects of Wife's Resources on Husband's
and Wife's Preferences for Wife's Outside Job
(husband employed, female respondents)

| | Percentage Desiring Wife to Work | | | | |
| | Wife's Preference | | | Husband's Preference | |
Housewife Families	Unadj.	Adj.	(N)	Unadj.	Adj.
Education of Wife					
Less than high school	29.8	27.2	(84)	10.6	11.5
High school	27.3	25.7	(128)	11.6	11.4
Some college	27.8	31.6	(54)	20.0	20.3
4 years of college	13.8	21.2	(29)	24.1	22.0
eta^2-beta^2	1.0	0.4		1.8	1.5
Significance	NS	NS		NS	NS
Working-Wife Families					
Education of Wife					
Less than high school	66.7	69.5	(36)	50.0	61.3
High school	83.9	84.3	(56)	55.4	54.9
Some college	86.4	87.8	(22)	50.0	48.2
4 years of college	96.2	90.1	(26)	80.8	67.8
eta^2-beta^2	7.0	4.1		5.1	1.6
Significance	.05	NS		NS	NS
Income of Wife					
Less than $3,999	84.2	87.3	(57)	38.6	43.7
4,000– 6,999	75.6	79.1	(41)	61.0	60.4
7,000– 9,999	85.7	82.7	(21)	81.0	77.0
10,000+	85.7	73.4	(21)	81.0	72.3
eta^2-beta^2	1.2	1.7		12.9	6.9
Significance	NS	NS		.001	.01
Occupational Status of Wife					
(High) 47+	90.0	84.8	(40)	72.5	53.3
37–46	85.7	85.0	(35)	62.9	57.0
24–36	71.0	73.1	(31)	54.8	68.6
(Low) less than 23	79.4	84.4	(34)	38.2	54.3
eta^2-beta^2	3.4	1.6		6.7	1.4
Significance	NS	NS		.05	NS

TABLE 3.5 (Continued)

Work Status					
Part time	89.6	85.3	(48)	37.5	42.9
Full time	78.3	80.5	(92)	68.5	65.7
eta^2-beta^2	2.0	0.3		8.9	4.8
Significance	NS	NS		.001	.001

sponded once again in a family utilitarian fashion, desiring the wife to work more the higher her educational level.

FAMILY LIFE CYCLE

For housewife families, the effect of family life cycle on role preference is unclear. Its effect on working-wife role commitment, however, is stronger. We see great pressure for the housewife to go to work in the prechild stage, a pressure not totally realized, apparently, in behavior. We see the same effect on commitment to work among both working wives and their husbands. For housewives, the effect of number of children is unclear, but there tends to be more desire to work among those with young children—evidence of a slight "trapping" effect. Working wives show less work commitment with young children present, but the important effect here is number of children. Working wives are less committed to work the more children they have. This is even more clear with perception of husband's preference. Thus, large numbers of children show a negative effect on desire for work by the wife *not* realized in behavior (see Chapter 2). ˙

At the "empty nest" stage, the wife's desire to work tends to increase somewhat, while her husband's perceived preference goes in the opposite direction. Again, a family utility versus personal satisfaction tension seems to explain the data best. In the prechild stage, it is best both for the wife's personal satisfaction and for family utility that she work; she would be bored at home with no children to occupy her and, even controlling for husband's income, extra income is needed to accumulate those assets—home, car, large appliances—needed for a comfortable family life. In the empty nest stage, however, she may once again become bored at home, but now the important assets have been obtained, house notes have been shrunk by inflation or have disappeared altogether, most major appliances have been purchased, the expense of children has been drastically reduced, and if she has stayed off the job market while her children were at home, she no longer has the job skills necessary to earn a good income. Once again, the husband's perceived preference reflects the family's utility, which, in the empty nest stage, may also be a strong reflection of his own personal satisfaction.

Those variables most closely tied to family economic utility—husband's income, housewife's education (as potential for income), working wife's income, and part- or full-time status—show a utility-predicted impact more on the wife's perception of her husband's preference than on her own. Her own preference seems to be impacted more by variables related to her personal satisfaction (as with working wife's education and occupational status, and her desires in the empty nest stage) and to be unrelated to utility variables. Her perception of her husband's preference might therefore best be characterized as the "voice of family utility." As we saw earlier (see Table 3.2), the wife's decision to work is a composite of both her own preferences and those of her husband (as perceived by her). Her choice of work role then, is a result of a complex interaction of her own desire for personal satisfaction and a desire to maximize that of her husband and family.

SEX-ROLE IDEOLOGY

The advocacy of nontraditional sex-role prescriptions and women's independence should have an effect on preference-role discordance. The predictor is straightforward. Advocacy of traditional roles means wife is housewife and husband is breadwinner ("A woman's place is in the home"). Advocacy of women's independence generally means the opposite, although, as we have seen (see Chapter 2), the two can coexist.

Table 3.6 shows the effects of the wife's ideology both on her preferences and those ascribed to her husband.[1] A housewife is significantly less likely to be satisfied with her position if she rejects the traditional, sex-based allocation of roles. The effects of the traditional sex-role scale and the women's independence scale are similar. For working wives, however, it is the traditional sex-role ideology scale that makes the difference. Women's independence beliefs make little difference, just as this scale was an extremely weak predictor of labor force participation (see Table 2.4) In addition, in no case does wife's ideology have a significant effect on husband's perceived preference.

As with wife's labor force participation, then, it is the advocacy of a certain system of roles, rather than general beliefs about women's independence, that makes a difference in preference for work. These beliefs make themselves felt not only in behavior, but as we see here, in those hidden preferences not fully explicated in action.

Again, as with the impact of the ideological variables on labor force participation, ideology has an effect on role preference indepedent of structural variables. Thus, the relationship of the family to the cultural system can be treated as an additional "contingency"—an additional characteristic of the environment to which the family makes structural adaptation.

EFFECT OF HUSBAND'S PERCEIVED PREFERENCE ON WIFE'S PREFERENCE

We have been able to identify wife's perception of her husband's preference as the "voice of family utility"—that is, as more responsive to the family's needs (which in many cases are at least partly equivalent to his own needs) than is the wife's preference. It then becomes important to ask the question: Do the wife's preferences respond to those of her husband, whether

TABLE 3.6   Effects of Wife's Ideology on Husband's
and Wife's Preferences for Wife's Outside Job
(husband employed, female respondents)

| | *Percentage Desiring Wife to Work* | | | | | |
| | *Wife's Preference* | | | | *Husband's Preference* | |
Housewives	*Unadj.*	*Adj.*	*(N)*		*Unadj.*	*Adj.*
Traditional Sex-Role Ideology						
Traditional	24.5	24.2	(151)		9.9	12.0
Nontraditional	29.2	29.5	(144)		18.5	16.2
$eta^2 - beta^2$	0.3	0.4			1.5	0.4
Significance	NS	NS			.05	NS
Women's Independence Ideology						
Traditional	23.6	23.0	(174)		12.0	12.9
Nontraditional	31.4	32.4	(121)		17.1	15.8
$eta^2 - beta^2$	0.8	1.1			0.5	0.2
Significance	NS	NS			NS	NS
Working Wives						
Traditional Sex-Role Ideology						
Traditional	68.2	68.9	(44)		52.3	56.3
Nontraditional	88.5	88.2	(96)		60.4	58.6
$eta^2 - beta^2$	6.1	5.5			0.6	0.1
Significance	.01	.01			NS	NS
Women's Independence Ideology						
Traditional	81.2	84.3	(69)		50.7	52.0
Nontraditional	83.1	80.0	(71)		64.8	63.5
$eta^2 - beta^2$	0.1	0.3			2.0	1.4
Significance	NS	NS			NS	NS

or not they can be identified with family utility? Put more simply, what effect does husband's perceived preference have on
wife's role preference, over and above the effects of the structural variables?

Table 3.7 presents the effect of husband's perceived preference with and without controls for structural variables, and

TABLE 3.7 Effects of Husband's Perceived Preference on Wife's Desire to Work (husband employed, female respondents)

Husband Wants Wife to Work	Percentage of Wives Desiring to Work			
	Unadjusted	Adj. for Structural Variables	Adj. for Structural Variables & Wife's Ideology	(N)
Housewives				
Yes	48.8	47.4	46.7	(41)
No	23.3	23.4	23.6	(254)
$eta^2-beta^2-beta^2$	3.5	4.0	3.3	
Significance	.001	.001	.01	
Working Wives				
Yes	82.7	82.8	82.8	(81)
No	81.4	81.2	81.2	(59)
$eta^2-beta^2-beta^2$	.01	0.1	0.1	
Significance	NS	NS	NS	

with additional controls for wife's ideology. For housewives, husband's perceived preference has a powerful effect on wife's role preference, and this effect is unchanged when the effects of the structural variables and sex-role ideology are controlled. This matching of preferences for housewives, then, is not a result of husband's perceived preference echoing family utility for wife's own ideology, but is instead an independent, powerful effect. Therefore, though her perception of her husband's preference seems to be related to the family's utility, it has a powerful independent effect on her role preference over and above family utility considerations.

For working wives, husband's perceived preference has no effect on wife's preference whatsoever, and this situation is not changed by controls. The working wife forms her own, independent opinion of her role preferences, whereas the housewife, more isolated from the world, and perhaps more dependent on her husband's view of it, tends to match her opinion to his.

In the introduction to this chapter, we asked two related questions. The first addressed the question of the impact of structural and ideological variables on role preferences not actualized in behavior. This question has been the one primarily addressed so far. The second, and related, question focused on the loci of the *tension* between role and preference—that is, on what structural conditions generate a feeling of "forcedness." This question has been touched on but not approached directly. Table 3.8 reworks the data presented in Tables 3.4 thru 3.7 by presenting values in terms of role discordance. Expressed in each category is the percentage of wives occupying a role other than the one they prefer.

We can generalize as follows: Role discordance is highest when husband's occupational status is low and when his education is low, when wife's education is low, when her income is relatively high (when she is working), before children are present, the younger the children are, and the more of them there are. Role discordance is also present when ideology conflicts with role and, for the housewife, when the husband wants her to work and she does not. In general then, except for the case of working wife's income, low family resources and high demand for them (as reflected in family composition) create pressures on the choice of family work allocation that lead to discordance between the role the wife occupies and the one she wants to occupy.

In this chapter we have found some residual effects of those variables linking the family to the socioeconomic structure. By residual, we mean variation in preference for a particular role not actualized in behavior. These variations in preference are partially explainable by the needs of the husband and family and by the husband's view of the ideal role for his wife. Other patterns—particularly variations in the wife's preference—are explainable by reference to the wife's need for personal satisfaction. It can be said that, in general, the ability to actualize preference in behavior depends on the resources of the husband

TABLE 3.8 Role-Preference Discordance Among Wives:
Effects of Structural Variables (husband
employed, female respondents)

	Housewives		Working Wives	
Husband's Education				
Less than high school	26.5	(88)	19.9	(29)
High school	34.7	(97)	17.6	(59)
Some college	14.7	(44)	19.8	(27)
4 years of college	23.5	(66)	14.1	(25)
beta^2 – Significance	2.3 – NS		0.3 – NS	
Husband's Income				
Less than $4,999	20.4	(20)	16.5	(21)
5,000– 8,999	34.9	(64)	11.7	(28)
9,000–11,999	28.6	(75)	21.1	(38)
12,000–15,999	16.9	(65)	21.9	(38)
16,000+	28.4	(71)	12.8	(15)
beta^2 – Significance	2.1 – NS		1.2 – NS	
Husband's Occupational Status				
High	21.7	(81)	6.5	(30)
Medium	28.1	(150)	16.8	(81)
Low	30.0	(64)	32.5	(29)
beta^2 – Significance	0.5 – NS		4.9* – .05	
Wife's Education				
Less than high school	27.2	(84)	30.5	(36)
High school	25.7	(128)	15.7	(56)
Some college	31.6	(54)	12.2	(22)
4 years of college	21.2	(29)	9.9	(26)
beta^2 – Significance	0.4 – NS		4.4 – NS	
Wife's Income				
Less than $3,999			12.7	(57)
4,000– 6,999			20.9	(41)
7,000– 9,999			17.3	(21)
10,000+			26.6	(21)
beta^2 – Significance			1.7 – NS	
Occupational Status of Wife				
(High) 47+			15.2	(40)
37–46			15.0	(35)
24–36			26.9	(31)
(Low) less than 23			15.6	(34)
beta^2 – Significance			1.6 – NS	

(continued)

TABLE 3.8 (Continued)

	Housewives		Working Wives	
Work Status				
Part time			14.7	(48)
Full time			19.5	(92)
beta^2 – Significance			0.3 – NS	
Family Life Cycle				
Prechild	35.2	(19)	32.6	
Age of youngest less than 6				
1	38.7	(37)	15.8	
2–3	25.8	(84)	22.6	
4+	28.0	(20)	40.2	
Age of youngest 6+				
1	24.1	(17)	0.0	
2–3	14.8	(45)	9.1	
4+	31.8	(19)	19.2	
Empty nest	26.7	(49)	16.6	
Childless	17.4	(5)	22.4	
beta^2 – Significance	2.5 – NS		6.8 – NS	
Traditional Sex-Role Ideology				
Traditional	24.2	(151)	31.1	(44)
Nontraditional	29.5	(144)	11.8	(96)
beta^2 – Significance	0.4 – NS		5.5* – .01	
Women's Independence Ideology				
Traditional	23.6	(174)	15.7	(69)
Nontraditional	32.4	(121)	20.0	(71)
beta^2 – Significance	1.1 – NS		0.3 – NS	

and wife. The lower the family's resources, the more any allocation of the work role will be experienced as forced. Put another way, the poorer, poorly educated, low occupational status families with heavy demands from children have only an array of bad choices available to them. Family work allocation may be at least partly a rational response to social and economic contingencies, but the "best" choice under the circumstances does not always bring satisfaction to the family's members.

NOTE

1. For a description and discussion of these two scales, see Chapter 2.

4

The Allocation
of Housework

Just as early attempts at explaining labor force participation ignored the marketwork contribution of the wife (both in economics and sociology), the assumption was common until very recently that housework could be *defined* as women's work. It turns out that in terms of hours spent in household chores, the evidence shows unequivocally that housework *is* largely women's work, whether or not the wife holds an outside job (Walker and Gauger, 1970, 1973; Walker, 1969; Gove and Peterson, 1980). The rapid increase in women's labor force participation in the last few decades has not brought about equality in the allocation of household chores between husband and wife.

Within this general tendency, however, there is variation, and a number of theories have been proposed to explain that variation. In economics, the most widely accepted model is that of Becker (1965) and others, in which the allocation of household tasks is treated as one aspect of the total allocation of time and can be explained by a model similar to that used to predict female labor force participation. Though the theoretical work has been carried out by a number of economists (Mincer, 1962; Gronau, 1973; Gramm, 1975; Leibowitz, 1975), there has been very little *direct* measurement of household task allocation by economists, and this is perhaps the most glaring omission in economic research on time and task allocation.

The sociological research on household task allocation has centered on "resource" theory (Blood and Wolfe, 1969; Heer, 1963) and on the effect of attitudes concerning sex-role behavior (Hesselbart, 1976). There is much less parsimony in the sociological approach to housework than there is among econo- mists. Sociologists, however, have been responsible for most data collection.

A detailed outline of the economic theory of time allocation was presented in Chapter 1. In brief, the wife is seen as allocat- ing her time between marketwork and leisure. The participa- tion of the husband and wife in these spheres of activity is determined chiefly by their relative productivities in market- work and household. The criterion on which the allocation is based is the maximization of the *family's* utility.

Sociologists tend to emphasize the "power" dimension of household structure, generally measured by participation in decision making. The explanation of task allocation is also tied to the notion of power, yet the theoretical base and the applica- tion of the power resource theory to household task allocation is rarely made clear. Some theorists seem to treat task alloca- tion as the result of a power relationship, and others as a meas- ure of power (see Farkas, 1975, for example). At one extreme, task allocation can be perceived as the "resolution of a power struggle over housework" (Blood and Hamblin, 1958: 350). Conceived in this way, the resources of partners enable them to reduce the hours spent in housework. On the other hand, the same researchers who see relative resources as important simul- taneously treat "needs" and "fairness" as important. For exam- ple, the explanation for the lower household task participation of wives when they hold a job, and particularly the higher level of participation of working wives' husbands, is based not only on their relative "resources," but also on the fact that certain tasks have to get done, the working wife has less time to do them, and therefore the husband pitches in. Certain passages in the sociological "resource" literature have a definite func- tional cast, implying that the wife works because her income is of more value to the family than is her total immersion in house- work, and naturally the husband compensates by increasing his participation.

The high frequency of "equal" responses to decision-making items in power structure scales has led some researchers to the view that, rather than being the outcome of a power struggle, task allocation is better characterized as "a smooth-working pattern of getting the necessary tasks done by whoever is available—without either partner feeling superior or inferior in power no matter who does what" (Blood and Hamblin, 1958: 351). As Heath (1976) points out, a person may not wish to take advantage of a strong bargaining position; it is a choice. The whole question of resources is a complex one. In Heer's (1963) elaboration of Blood and Wolfe's theory, he suggests that it is not just the value to one partner of the other's resources that determines power, but the value of those resources *relative* to those available outside the existing marriage. Thus, the greater the difference between the value to the wife of the resources contributed by the husband, and of the value to the wife of those resources which she might attain outside the marriage, the greater the power of her husband, and vice versa. When applied to task allocation, this would suggest that if the wife is employed and earns a high income or has a high education (and therefore has a high income potential), she is less tied to her partner and can demand a lesser share of housework as a condition for staying in the marriage. The husband agrees because her value to him (as a wage earner, for example) makes it worth his doing extra chores to keep her.

It is ironic that the economists—notable for their assumptions of personal profit-maximizing and rational, calculating behavior, and sometimes criticized for their "selfish" view of human nature—see family members as acting to maximize the *family's* utility, whereas the more "humanitarian" sociologists often see both decision making and task allocation as a power struggle between husband and wife. Though the family-utility orientation of economists was originally only a useful assumption (Mincer, 1962), later work (Becker, 1973) claimed to show that this assumption (that each family acts as it is maximized a single utility function) could be derived from the idea that "persons who care for each other are more likely to marry each other than are otherwise similar persons who do not" (Becker, 1973: 523).

Unfortunately, for our purposes, the economists' family-utility explanation of task allocation, especially the focus on the value of time, makes similar predictions to that of the "power" model. Resources that have a positive impact on the value of marketwork time, and therefore the opportunity cost of nonmarketwork time, will also tend to increase "power" according to the sociological model. Both the opportunity cost of nonmarketwork time and the power of a member of the dyad will tend to reduce participation in household tasks, and may even increase relaxation time if that time can be conceived of as productive in (the next day's) marketwork.

As we have pointed out, the chief deficiency in previous tests of the economists' model has been their failure to measure directly the allocation of household responsibility. The problem with the models of the sociologists is their failure to develop an integrated model of family task allocation and to test it in a multiple regression approach. This analysis brings together variables of concern both to economists and sociologists in a single model, and uses that model to predict measures both of the allocation of responsibility and the allocation of time between husband and wife.

The survey measured two dimensions of participation in household tasks: (1) the allocation of the responsibility for tasks between members of the family; and (2) the time spent by the respondent in housework and in relaxation, from which the allocation of time can be deduced.

Respondents were presented with a list of six household chore areas:

(1) cleaning the house;
(2) maintaining the house and yard, repairs, painting, mowing the lawn;
(3) caring for the children;
(4) preparing meals;
(5) doing the dishes; and
(6) paying the bills.

They were to indicate from a list who was primarily responsible for that task and who helped. The choices were respondent, spouse, children under 18, other friends or relatives living in the home, "landlord," "hired help," and "no one." Respondents were allowed to indicate as many "helpers" for a task as they wished, but only one choice was permitted for the "primarily responsible" category.

The distribution of responses for the sample (husband employed) is given in Table 4.1. Only the responses for husband, wife, and children under 18 are shown. (The participation of others, particularly in the "primarily responsible" group, was minimal.) The "primarily responsible" are broken down into those who are solely responsible for the task (that is, they receive no help) and those who receive help.

The table is quite clear on a number of issues. Though children tend to help with most tasks (particularly cleaning house and doing dishes), they are rarely primarily responsible for any of them. In only one group of tasks—the traditional male handyman and yard maintenance tasks—does the husband participate more than the wife. Husband and wife are about equally responsible for paying the bills. The other tasks show a heavy wife responsibility. This is particularly the case with the care of children, where wives in families with children are solely or primarily responsible for their care in 91.6 percent of the cases. The husbands, however, are more likely to help in this chore (73.9 percent) than in any other. In the other four tasks (cleaning the house, caring for the children, preparing meals, doing dishes), the wife is usually primarily responsible. The variation exists primarily in whether or not the wife receives help rather than whether or not she is primarily responsible for the tasks.

In short, the results are consistent with other research in showing a strong segregation of household tasks and a strong tendency for the wife to be responsible for most of them. In addition to the allocation of *responsibility* for household tasks, there is a separate dimension of *time* spent in housework. The time spent in child care, for example, is expected to vary sharply with the number and ages of children, while the responsibility for their care may not. Though allocation of responsibility should have an effect on time spent by family members on housework, the total amount of housework that must be performed varies by family composition, number of rooms in the home, the presence of labor-saving devices, and the tastes of

TABLE 4.1   Allocation of Household Tasks (husband employed, N = 962)

	Level of Responsibility (percentage)			
	Solely Responsible	Primarily[1] Responsible	Provide Help	Total Who Participate
Cleaning the House				
Husband	0.2	2.5	45.4	48.2
Wife	23.7	71.8	2.3	97.8
Children	0.1	0.6	27.3	28.0
Maintaining House and Yard				
Husband	14.9	61.1	11.1	87.1
Wife	1.8	11.5	41.9	55.3
Children	0.3	1.7	20.1	22.1
Caring for Children[2]				
Husband	0.3	4.8	73.9	79.0
Wife	9.0	82.6	4.8	96.4
Children	0	0.1	4.3	4.4
Preparing Meals				
Husband	1.3	3.4	38.1	42.8
Wife	37.3	56.9	3.2	97.4
Children	0	0.1	15.0	15.1
Doing the Dishes				
Husband	1.7	4.6	30.1	36.4
Wife	31.9	51.5	8.5	91.9
Children	1.8	6.4	17.7	25.9
Paying the Bills				
Husband	14.8	33.5	29.1	77.3
Wife	17.8	33.3	29.8	80.8
Children	0	0.1	0.2	0.3

NOTE: Participants other than husband, wife, and children excluded. Therefore, percentages in first two columns in each subtable do not add to 100.
1. Primarily responsible but receives some help.
2. Families with children at home under 18 years of age only.

family members. The economic theories of family role structure tend to focus on the allocation of time between market-work, housework, and leisure, and even detailed economic studies of the allocation of household chores (Leibowitz, 1975) focus on time spent doing chores rather than on assigned responsibility. In economic household time-allocation theory, hours spent on marketwork, housework, and leisure by wives are assumed to sum to a constant (number of hours). Since the dependent variable studied by economists is virtually always marketwork participation (as a yes/no dichotomy or as number of hours), housework and leisure tend to be lumped together, and often leisure time is ignored in models of time for wives (sometimes even in the general theory itself; see, for example, Gramm, 1975). Thus, marketwork participation tends to be explained in terms of family demand for housework and for the wages produced by outside work, but housework itself is not measured. The basic theory predicts that a rise in family income should produce an increase in the *family's* demand for both leisure and home-produced goods, as well as market goods (Mincer, 1962), but the distribution of the wife's time between leisure and housework is difficult to determine from the theory (see Gramm, 1975). One fact is clear, however: Employment by a family member should decrease his or her total time spent on housework and leisure (since the theory assumes that the sum of the three is a constant).

Sociologists tend to treat outside employment as a "resource" for a family member. The employed wife has greater bargaining power and can thus demand a lesser share of the housework. But it is also recognized that a decrease in housework by working wives can simply be a function of their scarcity of time. The basis of the sociologists' prediction that outside employment reduces the amount of time spent on housework is not the simple assumption made by some economists (Gramm, 1975), namely that hours in marketwork and housework leisure add to a constant. Rather, it is some notion either of power or fairness that explains the relationships.

We asked respondents to estimate the time they spend "doing work around the house" (preparing meals, shopping, running errands, doing things for children) on an average weekday. They were also asked to estimate the average hours per weekday spent "doing things for fun or relaxation," "working on a job, including going to and from the job," and the number of hours of sleep they get on an average weekday night. Economists have traditionally had difficulty in defining "leisure" (Becker, 1965), though it tends to be treated as nonproductive (either directly or indirectly) and to be time-intensive (that is, more consumptive of time than of goods). Though not held to be equivalent to "leisure" as traditionally defined, "hours in fun and relaxation" come quite close to what might be termed "active leisure," as opposed to "sitting around time." It is an indirect measure of time strain, though it should not be defined as "free" time, since all time involves cost.

These four time components (work, housework, relaxation, and sleep) were measured for each respondent and broken down by wife's employment status (see Table 4.2). The most striking result is the huge difference between the time the husband spends on housework, compared with the wife (even if the wife is employed); the drastic effect of wife's work status on her own level of housework; and the stability of the husband's housework time, whether or not the wife works. These results confirm not only the pattern of effect observed in other time-budget studies (see especially Walker, 1969; Walker and Gauger, 1970); and Szalai et al., 1973), but the time estimates themselves are quite close to those of other researchers. For example, Walker's 1967-68 Syracuse sample yielded an estimate of 8.1 and 1.6 housework hours for housewives and their husbands, respectively. The figures for this sample are 7.4 and 1.5.[1]

The husband's total time spent in labor (work and housework) is about the same, whether or not the wife works. In fact, for none of the four components of time is there a statistically significant effect (at the .05 level) of wife's work status on husband's time. For wives, however, the effect is significant for each time component. The correlation (not shown) between their hours of outside work and their hours of housework is −.40. The correlation for husbands, however, is virtually zero: +.02. Involvement in outside work has a strong, positive effect on the wife's total amount of work, however, indicating that her decreased housework time does not compensate for her hours of marketwork. The correlation between her hours of marketwork and total work hours is +.59. The effect of her hours of

TABLE 4.2   Husband/Wife Time Allocation and Wife's
Employment Status (husband employed)

Hours Spent On:	Housewife Families		Working-Wife Families	
Housework				
Husband	1.54	(226)	1.65	(186)
Wife	7.42	(297)	4.08	(140)*
Job				
Husband	9.52	(226)	9.21	(186)
Wife	0	(297)	7.34	(140)
Total Work				
Husband	11.06	(226)	10.97	(186)
Wife	7.42	(297)	11.43	(140)*
Relaxation				
Husband	2.65	(226)	2.70	(186)
Wife	3.16	(297)	2.28	(140)*
Sleep				
Husband	7.21	(226)	7.16	(186)
Wife	7.58	(297)	7.31	(140)*

*Difference between housewife and working-wife families significant at .05 level.

outside work on her hours of relaxation (−.14) and sleep (r = −.09) are much weaker, though significant at the .05 level. The time unaccounted for by these four components varies sharply by wife's work status (not shown). About six hours are at the .05 level. The time unaccounted for by these four components is six hours for housewives, but only about two hours for full-time workers. Though there is probably some variation in other activities, such as personal care, eating time, and the like, it is likely that much of this difference in unmeasured time may be accounted for by "idle time," that is, the just-sitting-around time that tends to make the housewife role more boring than other roles.

It has been argued that much of the housework done by nonworking women is unnecessary or at least very inefficiently done. The comparatively weak effect of her employment status on wife's hours of relaxation, and its powerful effect on hours doing housework, provides support for Wilensky's (1961: 53) assertion in another context that there is a "Parkinson's Law for Women," that "work expands so as to fill the time available for leisure." In addition, certain characteristics of the wife that make her a more valuable producer in the job world—intelligence, energy, motivation, and education—may also make her a more efficient worker in the home. In other words, there may be a kind of selection effect, despite the fact that husbands do not respond to wives' employment by increasing their time doing housework. Husbands of working wives may nevertheless (1) actually take more responsibility but do the work more efficiently; and/or (2) accept lower-quality home goods: a messier home, more TV dinners, and so forth.

Exactly how the composition of housework for the husband and wife changes when the wife is employed requires a look at individual task groups and the distribution of responsibility. Table 4.3 presents the results.

For those four tasks traditionally assigned to the wife (cleaning, cooking, dishes, and caring for the kids) the working wife remains primarily responsible in most families (93.9, 91.3, 78.6, and 89.9 percent, respectively), even when she holds an outside job. The chief effect of her outside employment on the allocation of these tasks is that she is substantially less likely to be solely responsible for them; she receives no help, especially from her husband. Her children are most likely to pitch in by cleaning house, though this may be simply cleaning up after themselves. Maintaining house and yard, typically a masculine task, is done primarily by the husband, but he only increases his participation by a little if the wife works. Paying the bills shows an almost equal distribution of responsibility between husband and wife, though her work status has little effect on who has primary responsibility. The task is more likely to be done by both husband and wife if she works; she is thus not more likely to take over the payment of bills, but she is more likely to have her hand in.

To obtain an overall measure of responsibility allocation, it was necessary to assess the distribution of the nature of responsibility across the six task groups for each family and for each

TABLE 4.3 Effects of Wife's Employment Status on Allocation of Household Tasks (husband employed, wife's age less than 65)

	Solely Responsible		Total Responsibility[1]		Total Participation	
	House-wife Families	Working-wife Families	House-wife Families	Working-wife Families	House-wife Families	Working-wife Families
Cleaning the House						
Husband	0.2	0.3	2.4	3.2	42.4	56.4
Wife	28.8	16.8	96.7	93.9	98.3	97.1
Children	0.2	–	0.7	0.8	28.1	28.2
Maintaining House and Yard						
Husband	13.6	16.7	75.0	77.0	86.2	88.4
Wife	2.4	1.1	15.5	10.9	59.4	49.3
Children	0.6	–	2.3	1.9	22.9	21.7
Caring for Children[2]						
Husband	0.5	–	4.1	7.2	77.9	80.7
Wife	10.6	5.6	92.3	89.9	95.9	27.1
Children	–	–	0.2	–	5.0	3.6
Preparing Meals						
Husband	0.9	1.9	3.3	6.4	36.1	47.1
Wife	44.0	27.6	96.5	91.3	98.3	90.1
Children	–	–	–	0.3	25.9	26.5
Doing the Dishes						
Husband	1.6	1.6	4.0	9.6	28.7	47.1
Wife	37.6	23.6	86.6	78.6	93.7	90.1
Children	1.6	2.1	7.4	9.3	25.9	26.5
Paying the Bills						
Husband	18.0	9.3	47.1	49.0	76.0	78.6
Wife	19.4	16.0	52.0	50.4	76.5	87.5
Children	0.4	–	0.8	0.3	1.2	0.3

1. Those solely responsible plus those primarily responsible who received help.
2. Families with children at home under 18 years of age only.

family member. A scale of responsibility with three values— sole responsibility, primary responsibility, and some participation—was constructed for each task for each family member. It was decided to focus on the husband and wife in subsequent analyses, both because they assume primary responsibility for virtually all the task groups in virtually all of the families, and because theories of task allocation focus almost exclusively on the marital dyad. The summary measures were constructed by assigning a value of 3 to those chores in which the respondent has sole responsibility, 2 for those in which he or she has primary responsibility, and 1 for those in which he or she helps. The scores for all the chores were then summed and an average score constructed. (If there were no children at home, the "taking care of children" chore was not included in the divisor.) The mean scores will be termed the Wife's Responsibility Score (WRS) and the Husband's Responsibility Score (HRS). The scores, then, can range from 0 to 3, with 0 representing the case in which the husband or wife participates in none of the housework tasks, and 3 indicating sole responsibility for every task. In addition, a relative task allocation score (WRS/HRS) was calculated for each respondent by dividing the wife's responsibility score by that of her husband.

In calculating the WRS and HRS scores, an interesting phenomenon appeared. In the questionnaire, respondents were asked to estimate not only their own household task responsibilities, but those of their spouse as well. For both housewife and working-wife families, the mean WRS score for female respondents was higher than for male respondents, and the HRS scores were lower. Also, the relative task allocation score (WRS/HRS) was higher for female respondents. Table 4.4 gives the different estimates for male and female respondents. All differences between male and female respondents are significant at the .001 level, and some are quite large, particularly in the case of the relative task allocation score. The female estimate of WRS/HRS among housewives, for example, was 75 percent greater than that of the male respondents.

Our first guess was that there might be sampling problems. In Chapter 2 we found that working wives were undersampled among female respondents, which was explained by the lower availability of working wives due to their heavy time and energy load. We suspected that those wives with a heavier household responsibility load—even within work status categories—

TABLE 4.4 Comparison of Household Responsibility Scores
Obtained from Male and Female Respondents

	Male Respondents		Female Respondents	
WRS – Housewives	1.79	(229)	1.93	(298)*
WRS – Working Wives	1.66	(186)	1.81	(140)*
WRS – All Families	1.73	(415)	1.89	(438)*
HRS – Housewives	1.01	(229)	0.80	(298)*
HRS – Working Wives	1.10	(186)	0.84	(140)*
HRS – All Families	1.05	(415)	0.81	(438)*
WRS/HRS – Housewives	2.18	(229)	3.82	(298)*
WRS/HRS – Working Wives	1.85	(186)	3.09	(140)*
WRS/HRS – All Families	2.03	(415)	3.57	(438)*

*Male-Female difference significant at .05 level.

might be more difficult to reach in a voluntary questionnaire. But the female respondents actually gave higher **WRS** and lower **HRS** scores than the males—exactly the opposite of what one would expect, given this kind of sampling difficulty.

We came to the conclusion that the problem was not sampling, but *perception*. A number of reasons for perceptual distortion suggest themselves. For example, the questionnaire did not define the precise nature of "help," whose meaning is subject to various interpretations. The skewed nature of household task distribution, despite the presence of a rather egalitarian general ideology in most families, coupled with the fact that this skewed distribution exists even when the wife works full time, suggests that there might be some guilt among husbands. As a result, they might tend to overstate their contribution and define as "help" activities that wives see as making no significant contribution. Definitional problems should be expected even without such intentional distortion. For example, is the husband helping the wife clean the house if he only cleans up after himself? It might be expected that such definitional questions would be resolved in favor of the respondent—that is, husbands see themselves as being more helpful than do their wives, and wives see themselves with more responsibilities than do their husbands.

More important, there would in general seem to be more difficulty in a respondent estimating the responsibility of other family members than in estimating his or her own. They may not even be fully aware of the range of household chores performed by one another. Clearly, male and female respondents must be studied separately in the following analysis.[2] The best solution seems to be to focus on each respondent's estimate of his or her own household responsibility (though both scores are presented in the tables). Such a focus seems justified by the results. In general, the model is a better predictor of WRS scores using the female sample and of HRS scores using the male sample. For WRS/HRS, the model works about equally well with either sample.

No matter who the respondent is, it is clear from Table 4.4 that the wife's responsibility level reacts to her employment status; the husband's does, too, but not as strongly. As was clear from analysis of the individual task groups, separate analyses (not shown) showed that the strongest changes produced by the wife's employment status occur in her level of sole responsibility and in her husband's overall participation level—particularly his helping behavior. Though wives show some decline in primary responsibility with labor market participation, only about half of that responsibility is absorbed by their husbands. The rest is taken on by other family members or by paid help.

The picture that emerges, then, is one of traditional allocation of task responsibility, even when the wife works. The shifts that do occur when she takes a job primarily tend to be an increase in helping behavior by the husband and others (children primarily) rather than a takeover of primary responsibility by other family members. The relatively small change in task responsibility introduced by wife's entry into the labor force contrasts sharply with her drastic reduction in time spent on housework (see Table 4.2). Her time is cut in half, but her responsibility score drops by only about 6 percent (using female respondents)! Clearly, the nature of housework must change when the wife is employed. As suggested above, the family accepts lower standards of housework when the wife works outside the home. In addition, the increase in family income produced by her market income enables the family to purchase goods and services to substitute for housework time. Housework is probably also performed much more efficiently by working wives, or perhaps by the husbands of working wives. In short, alterations in the nature of rather than the allocation of responsibility for housework may be the most significant result of the wife's participation in marketwork.

Having investigated the effect of wife' employment on the allocation both of responsibility and the time spent on household tasks, the next step is to study the efficiency of the structural and ideological model. In sociological resource theory, employment of the wife is treated as one of her resources, and often as the most important one. But other characteristics of the husband, wife, and the household itself will influence household task allocation to the degree that they increase the "bargaining power" of husband and wife. In Heer's (1963) formulation of resource theory, bargaining power conferred by any characteristic of a spouse can be determined by examining what effect that characteristic has on the partner's ability to equal or better his or her situation outside the present marriage. Thus, a working wife with a high income or a nonworking wife with a potential for earning a high income (because she is well educated or has extensive previous work experience) will have more bargaining power because she can make it easily without her husband. A high income and education for the husband, vis-à-vis that of his wife, should have a similar effect on his power.

As determined by resource theory, the effect of the presence, number, and ages of children on task allocation is not as clear. Though the wife generally retains custody of children after a divorce, the husband is often held legally responsible for their economic support. To the extent that one partner is more committed than the other to their children, and to the extent that that partner views a stable home as essential to the children's welfare, he or she will be in a poorer bargaining position, because maintaining the marriage will be more important to him or her than to the partner. This "principle of indifference" applies not only to children, but to other attitudes. A partner more committed to marriage as an institution, or one with a moral aversion to divorce, will similarly lack power relative to a partner with a lesser commitment. In a sense, then, the commitment of one's spouse to maintaining the marriage is a resource; that partner must do more than his or her share of household chores, for example, if he or she wishes to maintain the relationship.

Whereas sociologists have tended to treat household task allocation as a system separate from the wife's choice of outside work (although they are related), economists see the allocation of the wife's time between housework and marketwork as a single system. In some formulations, housework and marketwork are assumed to make up the entirety of the allocation of wives' time, so that leisure time is ignored or, more often, lumped together with housework in discussions of time allocation. One drawback of the comprehensiveness of the economic time-allocation model is that it has allowed economists to ignore direct measurement of the hours spent on housework and leisure, and to focus instead on marketwork participation as an indicator of a complete time-allocation system by assuming that the housework/marketwork total is a constant.

The following analysis treats those families in which the wife works separately from those in which she does not. In time-allocation theory, the allocation of the wife's time between housework and leisure can only be determined by the value (or prices) of each. As Gramm (1975) points out, the value of the housewife's time cannot be determined from the same model used to predict the working wife's time. Specifically, while the value placed by the family on the working wife's time can be determined by her wage rate, this tie is severed when she leaves the labor market and is determined by the husband's wage rate if he enters the home production process. Unfortunately, Gramm's development of this approach is unable to predict the housewife's allocation of her time between housework and leisure from her husband's wage rate (the theory suggests various contradictory effects). Similarly for the working wives, prediction is difficult because the family's demands for both home goods and leisure tend to be affected in the same direction by a number of variables. For example, a higher husband's wage rate, if it increases family income, also increases the demand for both home goods and leisure. An increase in the wife's wage rate may make her time spent on leisure and home production more expensive and *lower* the demand for them (in economics terminology, a "substitution effect"). Yet if her wages increase family income (if they are "uncompensated"), the increased rate has a positive effect on the family's demand for both. The relative effect on both husband's and wife's wage rates on the allocation of family members' home time must therefore be determined empirically.

In terms of the sociological resource model, treating wife-employed and wife-not-employed families separately is simply one method of controlling for the effects of wife's employment status in order to study the contribution of other resources to and the constraints on housework allocation. Wife's employment status is not controlled in a single regression analysis— that is, it is not entered as just another predictor—for two related reasons. First, the effects of the other predictors are somewhat different for families with employed than for families with non-employed wives: an interaction effect. Since regression analysis (including the form of dummy variable analysis used here) assumes that there is no interaction between predictors, including wife's employment status as a control variable in such an analysis would yield invalid results. Second, wife's income and occupational prestige are variables that are theoretically relevant predictors for working wives, but not for housewives. This might be termed "model interaction," a problem similar to the one Gramm (1975) encountered. For these reasons, it is best to study the wife-employed and wife-not-employed families separately.

In addition, such an approach will allow us to test the applicability of the economic time-allocation model to the allocation of household time between housework and leisure, given a certain level of marketwork. Since most of this theory is cast in terms of the allocation of time between marketwork and house-work, there is, as we have seen, some difficulty in drawing out predictions from the theory concerning housework-leisure allocation.

In the following analysis, the same general approach will be followed as in Chapters 2 and 3. The model used to predict housework allocation includes husband's resources, wife's resources, and household composition. Some of the "resources" variables are the measures of marketwork productivity used by economists, but variables of more relevance to sociological theories of task allocation are also included. Again, the effects of husband's and wife's ideologies on the allocation system will be studied. For the reasons outlined above, wife-employed and wife-not-employed families will be treated in separate analyses.

The sociological approach to household task composition tends to focus on the allocation of task responsibility between husband and wife. Economists speak of time allocation rather than responsibility allocation. Measures of both were obtained for the present study. However, the measures of time allocation were gathered for the respondent only, and male and female respondents will therefore be treated in separate analyses. Since the survey did not measure the allocation of respondents' spouses' time, husband/wife time allocation within any given family cannot be measured. The responsibility allocation variables (WRS/HRS), however, do apply to the dyad.

Our approach, then, is the same as that used to predict the wife's labor force participating. The variables linking the family to society's socioeconomic structure and to its cultural norms should be related to the allocation of household tasks. Again, the family unit adjusts its task and time allocation structure at least partly as a response to the social, economic, and cultural situation in which it finds itself.

As in Chapters 2 and 3, a dummy variable regression analysis was performed. A model combining variables of both sociological and economic interest was used to predict the measures of task allocation. To reiterate, the time allocation variables analyzed are husbands' and wives' hours spent doing housework on an average weekday, and hours spent doing things for fun or relaxation. As before, the measures of husband's resources used were his income, education, and occupational prestige. Wife's resources included education, for both the wife-employed and non-employed groups, and her income, occupational prestige, and part- or full-time status for the working group. A life cycle/family composition measure, including the presence and number of children, plus age of youngest child, was also included in the model.

HUSBAND'S RESOURCES

As in the two previous dummy variable regression analyses, the husband's resources or measures of his productivity—both economic and social—are his education, income, and occupational prestige. Again, only families with employed husbands were included in the analysis. Five dependent variables were used: three measures of responsibility allocation, and two of time allocation. The measures of the two components of non-marketwork time—hours spent on housework and on relaxation—were taken using the female respondents for wife's time and the male respondents for husband's time, since only the respondent's own time was measured in the survey.

The means given in Tables 4.5-4.7 for the values of each of the resource variables were adjusted for each of the other resource variables, and for the number and ages of children. These adjusted means should not be interpreted, therefore, as values expected in the population, but as values that would exist if the other resource and household composition effects were to be held constant. The pattern of means and the strength of the relationship thus give an indication of the independent effect of each variable.

According to resource theory, husband's educational level should be negatively related to his participation in household tasks. The economic theory of time allocation should predict the same results, since education increases the value of marketwork time more than the value of housework time. If, on the

TABLE 4.5 Effects of Husband's Resources on Household Task and Time Allocation, Adjusted Values (husband employed, wife not employed)

| | Housewife Families | | | | | | | | | | | |
| | Responsibility Load | | | | | | Time Load | | | | N | |
	WRS^4	WRS^5	HRS^4	$WRS/^4$ HRS^5	$WRS/^5$ HRS	$Wife^4$ HRS	Hus^5 $HSWK$	$Wife^4$ $HSWK$	Hus^5 $Relax$	$Wife^4$ $Relax$	Female	Male
Husband's Education												
Less than high school	1.97	1.78	0.73	0.97	4.14	2.36	8.03	1.37	3.59	2.60	90	75
High school	1.97	1.80	0.79	0.79	3.83	2.15	7.03	1.68	3.03	2.85	98	79
Some college	1.89	1.74	0.84	1.13	3.58	2.10	7.12	1.60	3.19	1.89	44	32
4 years of college	1.84	1.79	0.89	1.05	3.49	1.98	7.28	1.38	2.98	2.63	65	40
$beta^2$	1.6	0.4	2.0	2.5	0.4	0.8	1.6	0.6	1.1	2.0		

Husband's Income												
Less than $4,999	1.90	1.68	0.64	1.24	5.57	1.51	7.95	1.73	3.09	2.38	20	18
5,000– 8,999	1.93	1.75	0.83	0.96	3.42	2.20	7.86	1.56	2.92	2.33	65	42
9,000–11,999	1.90	1.75	0.85	1.09	3.52	1.86	7.72	1.54	2.93	1.98	75	49
12,000–15,999	1.88	1.88	0.89	0.97	3.14	2.64	6.71	1.52	3.35	3.34	67	56
16,000+	2.02	1.78	0.69	0.95	4.62	2.23	7.14	1.38	3.69	2.64	70	61
beta²	1.3	2.7	4.3[1]	5.9[2]	3.3[1]	4.5[1]	1.9	0.6	1.6	5.0[1]		
Husband's Occupational Status												
High	1.93	1.77	1.01	0.80	4.23	2.05	7.38	1.30	3.09	2.07	81	35
Medium	1.94	1.79	1.00	0.80	3.80	2.18	7.59	1.51	3.51	2.61	154	119
Low	1.90	1.79	1.04	0.82	3.23	2.25	6.99	1.62	2.65	2.82	64	72
beta²	0.1	0.1	0.3	0.1	0.8	0.2	0.5	0.6	1.9	1.3		

NOTE: Value adjusted for wife's resource variables, family's life cycle, and the other variables in the table.

1. Significant at .05 level.   4. Female respondents.
2. Significant at .01 level.   5. Male respondents.
3. Significant at .001 level.

other hand, husband's education is taken as a proxy for his ideology, it should affect household task allocation in the opposite direction, if we assume that better-educated husbands are more likely to favor female independence.

Overall, the ideology effect has the most consistent support. For the housewife families, there is a weak positive effect of husband's education on his responsibility, and wife's responsibility responds weakly in the opposite direction. Thus, the relative allocation of tasks between husband and wife clearly fits the ideology model, although the relationship is not strong.

The effect of husband's education on time allocation for housewife families is consistently weak and nonsignificant, and does not match the responsibility allocation results. Perhaps this results from a higher level of time efficiency in housework by better-educated husbands, so that more responsibility creates no change in actual housework time and no reduction in relaxation time. There may be more use of labor-saving devices by the husband if he is better educated, and his time may be more ordered and better used.

For working-wife families, the education of the husband has a weak though positive effect on his responsibility for household tasks. Others analyses indicate that his overall participation does not change appreciably, but that his level of primary responsibility does—that is, higher education shifts him from "helping" to "primary responsibility" in some tasks. The relationship of education to wife's responsibility is more complex and seems to be curvilinear, showing a heavy level of responsibility in families with husbands without a high school diploma, and a weak, positive effect of husband's education on wife's responsibility and time for the other educational levels. Other analyses seem to show a more specialized performance of tasks the higher the husband's educational level. The relative time-allocation measure is clear-cut for female respondents but unclear for male respondents. For the female sample WRS/ HRS is negatively related to the husband's education—a clear ideology effect.

The effect of husband's education on time allocation is weak and indeterminate for working-wife families, just as it was for housewife families. Again, the effect of education on efficiency in household production seems the best explanation.

Husband's income shows the same lack of a clear effect on task responsibility allocation for both housewife and working-wife families. It is generally curvilinear, with relatively high husband and low wife participation in the middle-income range, and vice versa in the low and high ranges. Such a curvilinear pattern suggests opposing forces at work, forces which themselves may not operate in a perfectly linear manner. The low level of husband participation at the low income levels may be an ideological or cultural effect. Related may be a compensation effect, where the husband compensates for his lack of success in the work world by enforcing the traditional sex-role ideology at home.

At the other end of the income continuum, we might expect a work-involvement effect, in which a high income is partly the result of heavy commitment of time and energy to a job at the cost of less home involvement. The wife is more willing to take on the increased burden, because the income increases the family's utility.

These two contradictory effects produce a curvilinear pattern, it is suggested, because they are not linear, but instead increase more sharply at the extremes of the income continuum. Specifically, the ideology effect increases sharply when the husband's income is below the sufficiency level, and higher-income occupations demand a heavy emotional as well as temporal involvement that causes the husband to retreat from home involvement. Such an explanation is quite speculative, however, and more analysis is necessary before a definitive interpretation can be made.

The time allocation measures for housewife families support the dual-effect interpretation. Hours in housework and relaxation for husbands show opposite curvilinear patterns by income. For wives, there is less of a tendency to curvilinearity and a much less pronounced increase in relaxation time at higher income levels, suggesting that although the housewife takes over responsibility from her husband at high income levels, his higher income enables her to purchase time- and

TABLE 4.6 Effects of Husband's Resources on Household Task and Time Allocation, Adjusted Values (husband employed, wife employed)

| | Working-Wife Families | | | | | | | | | | | |
| | Responsibility Load | | | | | Time Load | | | | | N | |
	WRS[4]	WRS[5]	HRS[4]	WRS/[4] HRS[5]	WRS[5]/ HRS	Wife[4] HRS	Hus[5] HSWK	Wife[4] HSWK	Hus[5] Relax	Wife[4] Relax	Female	Male
Husband's Education												
Less than high school	1.97	1.73	0.73	1.07	4.71	1.86	4.75	1.46	2.54	2.75	28	44
High school	1.75	1.63	0.85	1.09	2.80	1.87	3.79	1.78	2.00	2.55	59	66
Some college	1.73	1.67	0.83	1.10	3.09	2.15	4.11	1.40	2.43	3.05	27	40
4 years of college	1.85	1.66	0.98	1.18	1.88	1.47	4.75	2.03	2.70	2.27	25	36
beta[2]	5.4^3	1.0	4.2	1.3	8.5^2	2.1	2.2	2.8	3.0	1.4		

Husband's Income											
Less than $4,999	1.77	1.65	0.89	1.07	2.96	1.81	3.81	2.03	2.51	2.82	21	18
5,000– 8,999	1.80	1.67	0.83	1.08	2.76	2.07	5.13	1.97	2.48	2.69	28	58
9,000–11,999	1.72	1.61	0.91	1.18	2.24	1.75	3.94	1.64	2.20	2.85	37	44
12,000–15,999	1.87	1.75	0.80	1.05	3.62	1.90	3.68	1.32	2.05	2.50	38	43
16,000+	1.92	1.63	0.75	1.15	4.65	1.42	5.19	1.36	2.71	2.31	15	23
$beta^2$	3.0	2.0	2.2	2.1	5.6	1.9	4.6	4.1	1.8	0.7		
Husband's Occupational Status												
High	1.77	1.58	0.81	1.16	3.35	1.94	3.59	1.59	2.14	2.69	30	30
Medium	1.83	1.70	0.85	1.12	3.15	1.70	4.60	1.74	2.54	2.74	80	100
Low	1.78	1.66	0.86	1.05	2.63	2.07	3.82	1.58	1.88	2.46	26	56
$beta^2$	0.4	1.3	0.2	1.3	0.6	1.2	2.3	0.3	2.8	0.3		

NOTE: Value adjusted for wife's resource variables, family's life cycle, and the other variables in the table.

1. Significant at .05 level.   4. Female respondents.
2. Significant at .01 level.   5. Male respondents.
3. Significant at .001 level.

labor-saving devices and, in general, substitute market goods for home goods (eating out, hired help, and so forth), which allows her to make up time that would otherwise have been demanded by her increased responsibilities.

Time allocation among members of working-wife families is also roughly curvilinear for the wife and in the same way, though the pattern is not perfectly clear. Husbands tend to decrease both their housework time and relaxation time with higher incomes, suggesting a strong work-involvement effect.

Occupational prestige shows a very weak and consistently nonsignificant relationship to all measures of responsibility allocation, though it is clear that wives take on a greater percentage of responsibility the higher the husband's prestige.

In general, the husband's resource variables are more powerful predictors of responsibility allocation than of time allocation, and are more powerful predictors of responsibility allocation for working-wife families than for housewife families. Husband's education produces primarily an ideology effect, leading him to take more responsibility and his wife to take less at higher educational levels. Income shows a curvilinear effect, possibly the result of a combination of ideological-cultural causes at lower incomes and of time/energy overload factors in higher-income ranges. Occupational prestige contributes little to the model. For these variables, it is clear that a sociological concept (ideology) adds significant understanding to the relationships. The family is linked and must adapt not only to a socioeconomic but to a cultural system as well.

WIFE'S RESOURCES

For working wives, resources are measured by four variables: education, income, occupational prestige, and work status (part time or full time). For housewives, only educational status is relevant. All category means are adjusted for wife's resource variables, husband's resource variables, and the number and ages of children.

For housewife families, the wife's educational level has a postiive effect on both the level of her responsibility for household tasks and on that of her husband as well. The explanation for this relationship lies in the fact that the highly educated housewife is much more likely to carry out household tasks without help (analysis not shown). There is a slight tendency for the husband to increase his participation if the wife is highly educated (though his relaxation time increases significantly as well). This means that it is the participation of others outside the marital dyad that makes the difference.

Such participation is substantially higher for the more poorly educated housewife, and the help tends to be by others— mostly children. Education seems, then, to be positively related to the housewife's taking on slightly more responsibility for household tasks, though the relationship of this responsibility to her hours spent working is unclear. The husband also takes on more responsibility but spends less time at housework. There is less wife-skewedness in the allocation of responsibility, but the benefits seem to accrue to the husband, since wife's education has a powerful positive effect on husband's relaxation time.

The situation is rather complex for working wives. The effect of her education on her household responsibility and on the relative allocation of responsibility is quite strong, primarily because of the high relative responsibility in the high school-educated group. The negative effect of the working wife's education on her household participation supports the view that education increases the value to the family of her nonmarket-work time primarily; however, this energy seems to go into work involvement, since it is not reflected in relaxation time. Wife's income has a clearly negative and significant effect on her household responsibility and on her time as well, except that the highest-paid wives tend to have highly wife-skewed task allocation families, and this is somewhat reflected in her housework time. Neither the husband's time nor his responsibility seem to be much affected by wife's income, however. The

TABLE 4.7 Effects of Wife's Resources on Household Task and Time Allocation, Adjusted Values (husband employed)

| | Responsibility Load | | | | Time Load | | | | | | N | |
	WRS[4]	WRS[5]	HRS[4]	HRS[5]	WRS/[4] HRS	WRS/[5] HRS	Wife[4] HSWK	Hus[5] HSWK	Wife[4] Relax	Hus[5] Relax	Female	Male
Housewife Families												
Wife's Education												
Less than high school	1.85	1.81	0.84	0.96	3.88	2.13	6.76	1.56	3.31	1.96	85	69
High school	1.93	1.79	0.77	1.03	4.03	2.13	7.78	1.55	3.16	2.83	128	100
Some college	2.00	1.78	0.81	1.03	3.79	2.49	7.44	1.41	3.25	2.89	55	44
4 years of college	2.06	1.57	0.84	1.14	2.68	1.90	7.52	1.31	3.07	3.15	29	13
beta[2]	2.2	2.2	0.7	1.7	0.9	1.0	1.6	0.4	0.1	3.9[1]		
Working-Wife Families												
Wife's Education												
Less than high school	1.73	1.64	1.00	1.13	2.25	1.65	4.86	1.26	2.47	2.68	36	31
High school	1.96	1.70	0.75	1.10	4.15	1.94	4.30	1.81	2.13	2.61	55	97
Some college	1.70	1.71	0.79	1.08	2.35	1.81	4.32	1.72	2.88	2.66	22	32
4 years of college	1.67	1.54	0.87	1.11	2.57	1.81	3.08	1.58	2.08	2.77	26	26
beta[2]	10.5[3]	2.3	6.8[2]	0.2	7.7[2]	0.5	4.1	2.0	2.6	1.1		

											4	5
Wife's Income												
Less than $3,999	1.85	1.65	0.80	1.09	3.08	1.98	5.18	1.48	2.33	2.51	57	59
4,000–6,999	1.89	1.65	0.79	1.14	3.14	1.61	3.44	1.89	2.38	2.95	40	80
7,000–9,999	1.75	1.73	0.88	1.03	2.52	2.14	3.38	1.50	1.90	2.14	21	28
10,000+	1.57	1.74	1.03	1.12	3.56	2.00	4.00	1.58	2.57	2.58	21	19
beta^2	7.6[2]	1.0	4.9[1]	1.2	0.8	2.1	7.7[1]	1.8	1.3	1.8		
Wife's Occupational Status												
High	1.82	1.67	1.02	1.12	2.27	1.67	3.04	1.58	2.15	2.69	26	45
Medium	1.76	1.70	0.84	1.07	3.08	1.99	3.45	1.68	2.42	2.80	103	52
Low	1.84	1.59	0.77	1.16	3.44	1.70	5.39	1.76	2.30	2.21	61	38
beta^2	0.7	1.3	5.8[2]	1.1	1.8	1.0	12.6[3]	0.2	0.3	1.1		
Work Status												
Part time	1.84	1.79	0.86	1.00	3.22	2.42	5.65	1.61	2.46	2.66	48	50
Full time	1.79	1.62	0.83	1.14	3.02	1.64	3.68	1.69	2.24	2.65	91	136
beta^2	0.4	4.3[2]	0.1	3.1[1]	0.1	5.5[3]	6.4[2]	0.1	0.4	lt 0.1		

NOTE: Value adjusted for wife's resource variables, family's life cycle, and the other variables in the table.

1. Significant at .05 level.
2. Significant at .01 level.
3. Significant at .001 level.
4. Female respondents.
5. Male respondents.

wife's occupational status has a weak effect on her level of responsibility, but a clear negativ effect on wife-skewedness and a very strong effect on the time she spends on housework. Since the husband's time spent on housework and her own relaxation time also increase, however, there is apparently much less time spent on marketwork for the low-status working wife.

As might be expected, wives who work part time take on a heavier share of the chores than those who work full time. The relationship is not as strong as might be expected, however, relative to her other resources, an indication that it is not just hours of marketwork, but economic and social resources that make a difference, as well.

FAMILY LIFE CYCLE

The presence, number, and ages of children have a powerful effect on the allocation of task and time in the household. For both housewife and working-wife families, the presence and number of children reduces the wife's responsibility for housework but increases the amount of time spent at it, thus decreasing her time spent relaxing. The presence of younger children increases both her responsibility and time.

This decrease in wife's responsibility with an increased number of children is clearly not the result of the husband's taking on more tasks. If anything, he takes on fewer. The primary cause is that the children take on some responsibility. However, their pitching in by no means reduces the time needed for housework that is created by their presence.

The effect of children on the relative allocation of responsibility between husband and wife depends on the wife's work status. In housewife families, the presence of children brings about a decrease in wife-skewedness, but an increasing number of children brings about an increase. In working-wife families, the effect is precisely the opposite; the onset of children brings about an increase in the WRS/HRS ratio, but that ratio drops with a greater number of children.

For the housewife, then, children mean a sharp increase in housework. The wife takes the brunt of the increased demand for household goods, because her time is less "valuable" than that of the husband. The effect of having young children continues the effect it had on her decision not to join the labor force; it forces more and more involvement in housework. The value of the husband's marketwork time either stays the same or becomes more valuable when there are more children present. Their presence therefore tends to reduce or maintain his household participation.

The value of the working wife's time is higher than that of the housewife, yet in most cases lower than that of her husband's. The shifts in relative responsibility, though still in the husband's favor, tend, with increasing numbers of children, to reflect some increased participation of the husband in responsibility for household chores relative to that of his wife.

Overall, then, shifts in the allocation of household tasks and time tend to fit the family-utility explanation. Variation in household task and time allocation is a result of both the demand for household goods created by family composition and the value of the time of each spouse.

In contrast to the resource variables, the household composition predictor has a stronger effect on time allocation than on responsibility allocation, partly because children are the most important determinant of the total volume of housework demanded by the family, and partly because they complicate the responsibility-allocation picture. For the housewife, household composition is a far more important determinant of task allocation than are her resource variables. For the working wife, both are important. In general, the "full structural model," made up of the various resource variables and the household composition variable, does a substantially better job of predicting household tsk allocation for the working-wife families than for the housewife families. The greater amount of time unaccounted for (either by housework or relaxation time) indicates a less ordered and more amorphous allocation of time by housewives and, it is likely, much more variation in task allocation not accounted for by anything easily measurable. In addition, the husband's time allocation is much less predictable than that of the wife, largely because employed husbands simply do not

TABLE 4.8 Effects of Family Life-Cycle Stage on Household Task and Time Allocation, Adjusted Values (husband employed)

| | Housewife Families | | | | | | | | | | | |
| | Responsibility Load | | | | | | Time Load | | | | N | |
Family Life-Cycle Stage	WRS^4	WRS^5	HRS^4	HRS^5	$WRS/^4$ HRS	$WRS/^5$ HRS	$Wife^4$ $HSWK$	Hus^5 $HSWK$	$Wife^4$ $Relax$	Hus^5 $Relax$	Female	Male
Prechild	2.16	1.87	0.70	0.97	4.81	2.29	6.11	1.78	4.37	3.11	19	9
Youngest less than 6												
1	2.03	1.86	0.85	1.05	3.48	1.92	7.19	1.44	2.92	2.94	37	36
2–3	1.96	1.84	0.82	1.04	4.02	2.12	8.99	1.43	2.88	2.34	86	53
4+	1.72	1.78	0.83	0.95	2.49	2.21	8.58	1.53	1.80	3.16	20	19
Youngest 6+												
1	1.90	1.70	0.79	0.98	3.03	2.32	6.71	2.21	4.82	2.36	17	14
2–3	1.85	1.71	0.79	0.88	3.37	2.63	6.89	1.63	3.30	2.11	46	27
4+	1.73	1.54	0.67	0.77	3.99	2.55	8.21	2.00	3.67	2.36	18	11
Empty nest	1.98	1.76	0.82	1.11	4.56	2.07	5.37	1.29	3.35	2.72	49	50
Childless	1.93	1.83	0.97	1.12	2.85	2.12	6.00	1.00	3.00	2.29	5	7
$beta^2$	5.7^1	4.6	1.7	6.6^1	2.4	1.8	15.2^3	4.2	6.7^2	2.4		

Working-Wife Families

Family Life-Cycle Stage	1.99	1.69	0.91	1.19	3.30	1.54	2.50	1.13	2.69	2.56	16	32
Prechild	1.99	1.69	0.91	1.19	3.30	1.54	2.50	1.13	2.69	2.56	16	32
Youngest less than 6												
1	1.96	1.84	0.91	1.07	4.31	2.10	4.33	1.78	2.08	2.11	12	18
2-3	1.86	1.63	0.88	1.17	3.37	1.70	5.61	1.93	2.32	2.25	22	28
4+	1.45	1.42	0.68	1.23	2.67	1.31	3.43	1.75	1.57	3.00	7	4
Youngest 6+												
1	1.82	1.77	0.81	0.93	2.65	2.66	2.50	1.95	1.83	2.24	12	21
2-3	1.75	1.65	0.79	0.97	2.93	1.76	5.07	1.96	2.47	1.88	30	24
4+	1.50	1.23	0.68	1.14	2.45	1.25	5.90	1.73	2.00	2.27	11	15
Empty nest	1.92	1.80	0.87	1.08	3.15	2.17	3.46	1.56	2.63	4.03	24	35
Childless	1.57	1.49	1.17	1.36	1.79	1.27	3.20	1.44	2.20	3.44	5	9
beta²	15.9[3]	18.9[3]	6.3	9.8[1]	2.7	7.8[1]	16.9[3]	4.4	3.5	11.6[2]		

NOTE: Adjusted for husband's and wife's resources.

1. Significant at .05 level.   4. Female respondents.
2. Significant at .01 level.   5. Male respondents.
3. Significant at .001 level.

vary much in their time allocation, regardless of the pressures experienced by the family. Though they may take on more or less responsibility for tasks, the general tendency is to keep the time spent on housework constant.

SEX-ROLE IDEOLOGY

We expect sex-role ideology to be related to the household division of labor because beliefs in this area are specifically related to the "proper" roles of husband and wife. As described in Chapter 2, two ideology scales were developed, one focusing on the traditional allocation of roles between the sexes, the other on attitude toward women's independence in general. Since only the attitudes of respondents were measured, husband's and wife's collective ideology was entered in separate analyses, in each case adjusting for the variable that constitute the full structural model. The results are presented in Table 4.9. The effects of husband's sex-role attitudes are uniformly weak and nonsignificant. In working-wife families, the husband does spend significantly more time in relaxation and yet takes on a larger share of household tasks if he favors women's independence. Otherwise, his attitudes have no effect either on responsibility allocation or on time allocation.

The effect of wife's attitude, however, is stronger. It is also surprisingly complex. In general, wife's attitude has a significant effect on responsibility allocation only for housewife families.

For the housewife, endorsement of the traditional sex-role ideology is significantly related to a less wife-skewed allocation of responsibility, a relationship exactly the opposite of that expected. Endorsement of women's independence, though a weaker predictor, is also associated with a less wife-skewed responsibility allocation, as we would expect. The relationship of the working wives' attitudes to responsibility allocation is so weak as to be nonexistent.

Time allocation tells a different story. Here, the housewife families show weaker effects. Nevertheless, the effect of the traditional sex-role scale is also the opposite of that predicted.

The effect of women's independence ideology, though very weak, is in the expected direction; housewives who endorse it spend less time on housework and more time on relaxation.

Working wives' endorsement of the traditional sex-role ideology scale is positively related to their time doing housework, and negatively related to their relaxation time. The tendency to support women's independence is relatively strongly related to hours spent on housework, and in the expected negative direction. But it is also negatively and significantly related to hours spent on relaxation.

There are two possible explanations for the fact that endorsement of traditional sex roles leads to a lower level, both of time and responsibility for housework for housewives. The first is that the wrong causal direction has been posited. It is possible that endorsement of traditional sex-role ideology is a satisfaction response to a fair allocation system. When the wife feels overloaded by housework demands, she may reject the traditional allocation system that has created that overload. This is a kind of rebellion response that posits an effect from housework allocation to sex-role attitudes. This explanation, however, cannot deal with the effect of women's independence ideology, which runs in the *opposite* direction, especially for employed wives.

Another explanation, and one which seems more plausible, is that the endorsement of traditional sex-role ideology is an endorsement of a certain type of role allocation, rather than a direct endorsement of overload. Our summary measures of household task allocation include chores traditionally done by males (maintaining house and yard, paying the bills), chores that are "denied" to the wife under a traditional sex-based allocation of household tasks. Thus, though endorsement of the traditional ideology may cause the wife to take fuller responsibility for some chores, it may mean that she can safely abandon others to her husband. The overall effect may be to actually reduce her housework time.

The women's independence scale deals with the right of women to pursue roles—especially a career—outside the tradi-

TABLE 4.9 Effects of Sex-Role Ideology on Household Task and Time Allocation, Adjusted Values (husband employed)

Wife's Ideology	Housewives						Working Wives					
	WRS^4	HRS^4	WRS^4 HRS	$Wife^4$ HSWK	$Wife^4$ Relax	N	WRS^4	HRS^4	WRS^4 HRS	$Wife^4$ HSWK	$Wife^4$ Relax	N
Traditional Sex Role												
Traditional	1.85	0.84	3.33	7.33	3.53	152	1.76	0.81	2.64	4.21	1.91	44
Nontraditional	2.02	0.76	4.32	7.48	2.88	146	1.83	0.86	3.29	4.23	2.50	96
beta[2]	3.5[3]	1.0	1.6[1]	0.1	1.7[1]		0.6	0.2	0.9	0.1	2.7	
Women's Independence												
Traditional	1.98	0.77	4.05	7.55	3.26	175	1.83	0.83	3.16	4.78	2.71	69
Nontraditional	1.85	0.85	3.51	7.18	3.14	123	1.78	0.85	3.00	3.68	1.93	71
beta[2]	2.0[1]	1.0	0.4	0.3	0.1		0.3	0.1	0.1	3.5[1]	5.5[2]	

Husband's Ideology

Traditional Sex Role

Traditional	1.77	1.03	2.14	1.59	2.72	121	1.68	1.10	1.81	1.77	2.12	80
Nontraditional	1.79	0.99	2.23	1.42	2.44	105	1.66	1.10	1.88	1.59	3.05	106
beta²	0.1	0.3	0.1	0.5	0.4		0.1	0.1	0.1	0.1	4.4²	

Women's Independence

Traditional	1.80	1.01	2.24	1.43	2.62	143	1.73	1.05	1.97	1.75	2.39	94
Nontraditional	1.75	1.02	2.09	1.65	2.55	83	1.60	1.16	1.73	1.59	2.92	92
beta²	0.4	0.1	0.2	0.7	0.1		3.0²	2.8¹	0.6	0.3	1.5	

NOTE: Adjusted for husband's resources, wife's resources, family's life cycle, and the other variables in the table.

1. Significant at .05 level.   4. Female respondents.
2. Significant at .01 level.   5. Male respondents.
3. Significant at .001 level.

tional housewife role. The result, as Table 4.9 shows, is that an independence-endorser devotes more energy to marketwork and significantly less to both housework and leisure.

In summary, then, it appears that the endorsement of the traditional allocation of sex roles can be of positive value to the housewife because it can enable her to avoid stereotypically male tasks and perhaps to reduce slightly her total housework time. Endorsement of traditional roles is an impediment to working wives, however, and slightly increases the time they spend doing housework. Their endorsement of female independence chiefly increases their involvement in marketwork, and this reduces time spent both on housework and leisure. Overall, it is the wife's attitude that makes the difference in task and time allocation; her husband's feelings have little impact.

The results of this analysis are clearly not a full endorsement either of the sociological or economic explanations of household task and time allocation. Characteristics of the husband and wife that count as "resources"—whether these resources are associated with power or with the value of time—also link the dyad into a social-cultural, as well as an economic, system. The effects of certain variables often cannot be adequately explained without reference to the cultural situation in which income, education, and occupation status tend to place individuals.

The clearest result of the analysis, however, lies in the inflexibility of the time the husband spends on housework tasks. Shifts in responsibility and in housework time allocation are thus limited by this factor.

NOTES

1. It is probable that part of the difference in housework time for wives (0.7 hours) can be attributed to somewhat different methods of measurement. Walker's estimate was a sum of time spent on a number of different household chores, whereas we asked respondents to simply estimate total housework time. The slightly higher estimate obtained by Walker may be due to respondents counting certain areas of chore overlap in the same time period twice—that is, if two activities are performed simultaneously

(fixing dinner and cleaning up, for example), that same time period will be counted twice if the total time for each activity is measured separately and then summed. We have no evidence that this is the case, though it seems a plausible explanation.

2. For any predictor variable where the male respondent and female respondent distributions were not similar (for example, if families with young children were underrepresented among female, relative to male, respondents), the effect of the predictor variable would be biased when used in the analysis.

5

The Quality and Viability of Marriage

This work began with the assertion that attention to the functionality of work-housework role structure involves not just analysis of its causes, but of its effects as well. Though the model developed to explain work-housework role structure was based on the notion that such structures evolve as a semi-rational response to contingencies both in the external environment and within the family itself, it was proposed that the utility of such evolved structures should be treated as an empirical question rather than as an assumption. Ideology, habit, inertia, and ignorance also have their impact on behavior in the real world. In addition, a rational choice may be a choice among bad alternatives; in some situations families may be in trouble no matter what they do, at least within the limits of cultural restrictions.

At bottom, the functionalist argument rests on the notion of the *viability* of the family unit—that is, its potential for continuing existence. To use an economic analogy, the viable family is the firm that continues to exist because it continues to make a profit. When its efficiency is so poor that it is no longer profitable for the owners (members), it will be dismanted.

In the functionalist perspective outlined in Chapter 1, viability refers to the probability of marital dissolution. The most direct way to measure this probability is by measuring *marital stability*: the rate at which marriages end by the natural death of a spouse rather than by divorce, separation, desertion, or annulment (Lewis and Spanier, 1979). There are two reasons why this approach is unsatisfactory, one methodological and one theoretical. Such a study could be done in two ways: (1) a panel analysis, in which families are studied at one point in time and then followed until they dissolve through divorce or separation; and (2) retrospective interviewing of a matched sample of divorced/separated and nondivorced/separated families to determine their role structures—for the divorced/separated, the role structure prior to separation. Both approaches involve problems, the first primarily one of resources (such a study, even on a small scale, would likely be very expensive) and tactics (the difficulty of following families in such a highly mobile society, and the problems of the bias introduced by selective experimental mortality). The problems of the second approach are primarily perceptual, the same kinds of problems introduced by any retrospective survey. This is not to say that both kinds of studies should not be performed—they would each provide valid and important information—but that they each have their own kinds of serious problems.

The second and most important problem in using divorce or separation as a measure of viability is theoretical. Marriage is not simply a legal form or contract. As it is used by most researchers, and as it is viewed by the lay populace, marriage also refers to an ongoing *relationship* between two people. Two trends in American society emphasize this difference in perspective. The first is the growing number of individuals living in a heterosexual, stable family relationship without benefit of a formal contract. The second is the increasing liberalization of divorce laws and the acceptance of "no fault" divorce such that legal divorce is treated less and less as the legal ending of a relationship and more and more as a legal certification that a relationship has ended.

If marriage is defined as a relationship rather than simply a legal status, it becomes possible to treat the legal certification aspect and the relationship aspect separately. This then implies both that a marriage relationship can cease to exist without divorce (we might call this "uncertified divorce") and that it can continue to exist without marriage (stable couples "living together"). Such an approach also allows us to treat the marriage relationship as a continuum, or better, as a number of types of bonds between two people, the strength of which can be measured along a contiuum. In general terms, an analysis of the "functionality" of an organism's (family's) structure entails not only the potential for continued existence but the potential for continued *healthy* existence. In one sense, the choice between marital stability and marital quality as a measure of viability is a moot question, because there is strong evidence that the two are usually correlated (Lewis and Spanier, 1979).

The focus of the sociological research on marriage, particularly prior to the 1960s,[1] was on what was variously termed marital happiness, satisfaction, success, or adjustment—a subjective feeling about the state of marriage—or on marital stability, measured negatively by divorce or postively as cohesiveness. Since our central term, "viability," contains elements of both marital quality and marital stability, the relationship between these two general concepts and their history in the literature is vital for a proper treatment of viability. A brief theoretical and empirical investigation of the nature of marital viability is necessary for the analysis central to this chapter: the relationship between work-housework role allocation and the viability of the marital relationship.

The long history of attempts to measure the overall quality of a marriage has resulted in a situation where there are so many connotations to terms like happiness, adjustment, success, and satisfaction that no researcher can generate a consensus about the definition of any one. The introduction of new terms tends to magnify rather than solve the problem. Lively (1969) advocates the abandonment of all these terms. A number of researchers (Lively, 1969; Burgess and Wallin, 1953; Luckey, 1964) have pointed out that terms like "happiness" and "satisfaction" have different meanings not only for different researchers, but for different interview respondents themselves. Husband and wives, for example, often do not agree about the happiness of their marriage (Lively, 1969). Satisfaction can exist for either husbands or wives under a wide range of circumstances, such as cohesiveness, incompatibility, or unsolved problems of adjustment (Burgess and Cortrell, 1939). Satisfaction may be seen as applying to the spouse, to the marriage as a whole, or to one's life since being married. "Adjustment" and "success" encounter similar definitional and measurement problems. Indeed, in many cases these terms seem to be used interchangeably by researchers (Lewis and Spanier, 1979).

These kinds of problems are inevitable when one attempts measures of anything at a global level. Terms such as happiness and satisfaction cause definitional problems for researchers for the same reasons they cause measurement problems in surveys; such terms are inevitably measures of some combination of vague positive and negative affects toward one's situation and one's spouse. Such feelings are important social data in their own right, as studies of both general happiness (Gurin et al., 1960) and satisfaction (Campbell et al., 1976) have shown. The solution to definitional difficulties lies not in abandoning general, global measures such as these, but in (1) studying interrelationships between a variety of such measures in an attempt to better investigate their meanings; and (2) simultaneously measuring more specific components of relationships.

Thus, it is important not to pursue the evolution of some ultimate measure of the marital relationship which somehow supersedes all these different shades of affect, but to treat feelings of satisfaction, happiness, and the like as important and worth being studied in their own right. Therefore, the following analysis will not center on a single measure of the marital relationship, but rather on a variety of measures. These will include global, generalized measures of affect toward one's marriage and one's mate, measures of satisfaction with the role choices that spouses make, measures of the nature and quality of the bond within the dyad, and measures tapping the behavior that actually characterizes the relationship.

AFFECTION AND INSTRUMENTALITY

This initial sorting out of the various measures of marital affect and behavior can be started by making a distinction common in the literature. Researchers have long made a distinction between the *institutional* marriage and the *companionate* marriage, a distinction first pointed out by Burgess and Locke

(1945). A similar distinction between the "parallel" and the "interactional" type of marriage was made by Gurin et al. (1960). The institutional marriage is characterized by instrumental bonds between husband and wife. Roles are traditional, sex-segregated, and complementary—that is, to use Durkheim's terms, the locus of solidarity is organic rather than mechanical. This kind of marriage is that described, for example, in the early structural-functionalist approach, wherein the husband's role is primarily to provide for the material and status needs of the family, and the wife's role is expressive and integrative. His provision of needed goods and status is the primary determinant of the family's success. His wife provides integration and support in response to his satisfactory performance (see Scanzoni, 1970, for a detailed development of this approach).

The second type of marriage, the companionate, is believed to be growing in frequency, though the institutional marriage is still seen as the modal type (Hicks and Platt, 1970). This type of marriage places greater emphasis on the affective aspects of the relationship. Expressions of love by both spouses, and positive patterns of close interaction determine marital happiness. Though often treated as two distinct types, many researchers have pointed out that some aspects of instrumentality are important in companionate marriages, and that affection is important in the institutional. As with most typologies, the types are a reduction of what are admittedly continuums.

The instrumental and affectional continuums can be usefully treated as two types of bonds linking the marital dyad, and thus as crucial indicators of the strength and viability of the family unit. If we dichotomize each continuum for discussion's sake, we see that a correct specification of "types" of marriages involves at least four categories rather than two. These four product spaces (see Table 5.1) show that the relationship between bond strength and marital viability can be predicted in only two of the spaces. Viability can be predicted to be highest in those marriages high in both instrumentality and affection, and lowest in those low on both.

Empirically, the relative importance of these two kinds of bonds can be determined only in the discordant categories.

TABLE 5.1   Instrumental and Affectional Bonds

| | Strengths of Instrumental Bond | |
	High	*Low*
High	Highest Viability	?
Low	?	Lowest Viability

Though the institutional (instrumental) and companionate (affectional) marriages are usually treated as at least somewhat distinct types, the distinction between types can actually be made only when the affectional bond is strong and the instrumental bond weak, or vice versa.

An additional complication now arises. "Bond" implies a relationship—that is, a single "thing" existing between two elements. But in fact, instrumentality—the provision of material goods and services and status—and affection are directional. One can give either without receiving it in return, and vice versa. Thus, just as the perception of happiness or satisfaction in marriage is specific to each partner, the giving and receiving of material or status goods and of affection are specific to an individual rather than a relationship.

With these caveats in mind, the survey attempted to measure the perception of his or her *partner's* provision of both affectional and instrumental satisfaction. Respondents were asked the following questions:

Here is a list of some things people say are important for a good marriage. Please call off the letters of the items which describe the ways, if any, in which your husband/wife is very good.

(A)   Showing tenderness and affection
(B)   Companion
(C)   Sexual partner
(D)   Taking care of the house
(E)   Member of the community
(F)   Managing money
(G)   Host

(H) Earning a good living
(I) Understanding my problems
(J) Good moral character

Since more than one response was allowed, all responses were combined to produce scales measuring affection and instrumentality. The Affection Scale was created by summing items A (showing tenderness and affection), B (companion), C (sexual partner), and I (understanding my problems). These items provide a range of types of affection, both emotional and physical. The Instrumentality Scale was composed of items D (taking care of the house), E (member of the community), F (managing money), G (host), and H (earning a good living). These items tap the provision of material needs (F and H), services (D and G), and status (E). Our measure of instrumentality takes into account the recently popular realization that the wife's work (taking care of the house) may be just as "instrumental" to the husband as is his dollar income to the wife. The Instrumentality Scale is thus indicative of overall nonemotional need provision and is not limited a priori to those materials, services, and status needs provided only by the outside worker. The husband may be just as tied to his wife because she runs an excellent home as she is to him because he is a good provider.

It turns out that the Affection Scale is very skewed. Other researchers have found that, in general, responses of married people to items concerning love and affection tend to give strongly positive responses. For example, in our questionnaire, about 98 percent of the married respondents in the husband-employed subsample reported that "love" was "important in keeping (my) marriage together." The Instrumentality Scale is not so skewed. The skewedness of the Affection Scale means that in order to dichotomize it (the range is 0 to 4) at approximately the median, scores 0, 1, 2, and 3 had to be collapsed together. Thus a "high" Affection score means a perfect score, while a low score implies all other values. The Instrumentality Scale (range 0 to 5) was cut between scores 2 and 3.

When combined, these two scales yield a four-category variable. Table 5.2 gives the distribution for male respondents

TABLE 5.2   Affection and Instrumentality Scores, by Sex
               (husband employed)

	Male Respondents (Wife's Performance)		Female Respondents (Husband's Performance)	
	N	%	N	%
High in Both	140	(30.0)	120	(23.4)
High in Affection Only	134	(28.8)	137	(26.8)
High in Instrumentality Only	25	(5.4)	44	(8.6)
Low in Both	167	(35.8)	211	(41.2)
	477	(100.0)	512	(100.0)

(who judged their wives' performance) and female respondents (who judged their husbands'). Surprisingly, the distribution of the AI cateogires is remarkably similar for husbands and wives. Contrary to traditional structural-functionalist theory, there is little difference in the perceived instrumental and affectional roles of husbands and wives as perceived by their spouses. Overall, 35.4 percent of the wives versus 32.2 percent of the husbands scored high on the instrumentality measure, an indication that when non-job-related instrumentalities are taken into account, wives make an equal contribution to that of their husbands, despite the fact that nonworking wives are also included, for some of which "earning a good living" is a logically impossible characteristic.[2]

POSITIVE AND NEGATIVE INTERACTION

This AI variable measures the nature and strengths of the marital bond in general terms. Another important dimension of marriage is the behavior that is itself characteristic of a relationship. Recent researchers, particularly Orden and Bradburn (1968), have attempted to tap the positive and negative activities typical of the marriage relationship. They constructed two scales, one consisting of pleasurable activities (for example, "being affectionate toward each other," "visiting friends together") and the other of sources for disagreement (for example, "being tired" or "irritating personal habits"). The items measuring pleasurable activities were divided into a Companionship Index and a Sociability Index. The "areas of disagreement" items were summarized into a Tension Index. The authors found that while the two satisfaction scales were related to each other (.34 for men and .37 for women), neither scale was related to the Tensions Index. Thus, two separate and independent dimensions—satisfaction (pleasurable activities) and tensions (area of disagreement)—were found.

In the Orden and Bradburn study, each dimension was moderately related in the expected direction to a measure of overall marriage happiness. The authors combined two dimensions (the measures of satisfactions and tensions) into a "Marital Adjustment Balance Scale," and its relationship to their measure of marriage happiness (gamma) was .47 for the full sample (.44 for men .50 for women).

In the construction of our measures of positive and negative marriage affect, we borrowed many of the Orden and Bradburn items. From the satisfaction scale, we eliminated mainly those items that involved activities requiring the expenditure of money, and others that might have introduced a class bias.[3] Following Orden and Brandburn's (1968: 724) suggestion, we combined the companionship and sociability measures to create an overall positive interaction measure. Other items were deleted from the tensions measure either because they were obvious opposites to a positive item ("not showing love" versus "being affectionate toward each other") or because they received a low level of agreement on Orden and Bradburn's sample. Summing the items in both scales' yielded a Positive Marital Relations Scale and a Negative Marital Relations Scale. Just as Orden and Bradburn found, our scales also turned out to be virtually unrelated ($r = -.05$ for men and $-.09$ for women).

GLOBAL MEASURES

In addition to the positive and negative relations scales, a number of global indicators were included in the questionnaire: (1) Marital Happiness (Taking all things together, would you say your marriage is very happy, pretty happy, not too happy, or not at all happy?); (2) Marital Closeness (How close are you and your husband/wife—very close, etc.); and (3) Desire to Stay Married (At the present time, how much do you want to stay married—very much, etc.). Marital happiness is widely used and perhaps the most general measure of affect. Marital Closeness is intended as a measure of a relationship—specifically, overall marital bond strength—rather than of an individual's feelings toward the relationship. Inevitably, how close the respondent feels to his or her spouse may differ from the spouse's feelings. The third measure, Desire to Stay Married, is thought to be a good measure of marital stability—a direct measure of the "potential for continuity." Thus, these global measures offer a range of specificity and of affect.

Our primary focus of interest is to investigate how the viability of a marriage is related to its work-housework role structure. Work-housework allocation structure is conceived as performing a creative function for the family, converting possibilities into consumable realities. As family circumstances change, possibilities change, and role structure must change to maximize the family unit's utility in light of the contingencies—both of the external and internal environment—that it faces. Those role structures involved are only semi-rational (that is, sometimes irrational), however, and the extent to which a role structure contributes to a viable marriage depends on the mesh between the role structure and the environment. The measurement of viability, as we have seen, is a complex problem. It involves, at the most concrete level, satisfaction of the husband and wife with the roles they occupy. At the next level of abstraction, we are interested in the effect that work-housework role structure has on the nature and strength of the marital bond itself, given the external and internal conditions in which the family finds itself. Lastly, we are interested in more global indicators, which in their very vagueness may be good indicators of overall viability.

The investigation of such questions is a large task. Since we propose that a given work-housework structure will have different effects on marital viability under different circumstances, we are faced with the measurement of a specification or interaction effect. Since the possibly relevant circumstances are almost limitless, the measurement of such circumstances—that is, the creation of groups "in similar circumstances" for statistical analysis—necessary involves gross collapsing of categories and limitation to only a very few circumstances variables. Only in this way can subsamples of sufficient size be maintained so that the relationship between work-housework structure and viability can be determined *within* family circumstance subsamples with some degree of reliability.

MEASUREMENT OF CIRCUMSTANCES: INCOME AND FAMILY LIFE CYCLE

Two variables were chosen to create gross circumstances subsamples: family income and family life cycle. Family income is an adequate measure of the family's overall standard of living and an indicator of social status. In economic theories of labor force participation and time allocation, family income is a predictor of the family's consumption of both home goods and leisure. It is also a measure of the extent to which market goods can be substituted for home-produced goods, as well as being the best single measure of the availability of role alternatives for family members. If the wife is working outside the home, she may buy off housework time and substitute market goods and services. If the wife is not employed, she is under no constraint to work.

In terms of its direct effect on marital quality, the literature strongly supports the finding that socioeconomic status is a powerful positive predictor of divorce rates, and of marital quality as well (Lewis and Spanier, 1979). Its strong effects, both on work-housework role structure and on marital satisfaction, argue for its adoption as a key family circumstance variable.

The same can be said of the other circumstances variable, family life cycle. Our own results (Chapters 2 thru 4) show that this variable has strong effects on the choice of work role, and on the allocation of both responsibility and time for housework. It is thus a particularly salient indicator of "inner circumstances," those pressures exerted on the family from within. In addition, there is a growing literature on the relationship of family life cycle to marital adjustment and satisfaction (see particularly Rollins and Feldman, 1970; Rollins and Cannon, 1974; Spanier et al., 1975). Though the issue is not yet resolved, results provide some support for a curvilinear pattern (Spanier et al., 1975; Gove and Peterson, 1980). It is clear that marital adjustment drops sharply with the advent of children. It is less clear that it rises again after children have left the home.

Thus, family income seems to be the best single indicator of external contingencies, and family life cycle of inner contingencies. Collapsed versions of these variables will therefore be used to generate the family circumstance subsamples. It should be emphasized that this approach is only a preliminary one necessitated by the size of an average national sample. Further work with much larger samples could carry the specification of circumstances to a much more detailed level, possibly using educational status of husband and wife, number of children, occupational prestige, and ideological measures.

FOCUS: WIFE'S WORK ROLE

In the following analysis we focus on the wife's choice of work role as our indicator of work-housework allocation. As the analysis in Chapter 4 demonstrated, this variable has substantial impact on the way housework time is used, organized, and allocated. It is the most important way families adjust to the social and economic contingencies that confront them, and thus should be the key indicator of successful adaptation to those contingencies.

The analysis proceeds in a number of steps. Eight different subsamples classified by family life-cycle stage and family income are created. Within each subsample, the efficiency of two types of work-housework allocation schemes—housewife families and working-wife families—are compared in terms of the marital quality of each type of family within that group. These comparisons in terms of marital quality proceed from the most specific—discordance between role preference and actualized role—to the most general. Measures of quality include next the nature and strength of the marital bond, the quality of activities that characterize the relationship, and an overall assessment of the marriage by each partner.

PREFERENCE-ROLE DISCORD
AND FAMILY CIRCUMSTANCES

We move first to the most concrete measurement of marital quality: satisfaction of each spouse with the particular work-housework role arrangement. Again, for methodological rather than theoretical reasons (see Chapter 2), we focus on the wife's choice of the outside worker role. Specifically, we are interested in discordance between the work-housework role allocation scheme that exists and the one she and her husband would prefer. Such preference-role discord is measured in three ways. First, using the variable treated as dependent in Chapter 3—the wife's desire for outside work—we created a role-preference discord measure just as we did in that chapter. This preference-role discord variable indicates discordance between the wife's desire for work and her work status, whatever each is.

Second, preference-role discord for the respondent's husband was measured using her perception of her husband's preference. If the wife saw the husband as wanting her to work when she didn't or as not wanting her to work though she did, the husband was scored as discordant. These variables, of course, were also treated as dependent, as in Chapter 3. Ideally, we would want the husband's own statement of his disagreement with his wife's work role, but as we have pointed out, those data are not available. We must therefore settle for the wife's perception of the husband's disagreement with her work status.

In addition to the preference-role discord of the wife and her husband over her work status, preference-role discord for the allocation of housework responsibility was also measured. After each respondent had given a breakdown of the allocation of responsibility for household tasks (those variables studied in Chapter 4), he or she was asked: "Taking everything together, do you feel you do more than your share of household chores?

(Yes/No)." This direct measure of personal dissatisfaction with household task allocation and the two preference-role discord measures for the housewife's work role are broken down by family income and life cycle in Table 5.3. Working-wife and housewife families are presented separately for each family condition subsample.

Family income is divided into two categories: those families with total income above $12,000 a year, and those below. The patterns are interesting. For females in lower-income families, preference-role discord is generally lower when children are present and higher when they are not. The pattern is generally the opposite for upper-income women.

Before any children arrive, both lower- and upper-income women experience less preference-role discord when they work. The same is true of the husband. When young children are present, there is virtually no difference in dissatisfaction between working and nonworking women. Though the difference is not large, housewives tend to be somewhat more satisfied than their working counterparts when families are older. The husbands show much more discord when their wives work when children are present. In the empty nest stage, the low-income wives have about equal preference-discord levels no matter what their work status, whereas upper-income wives seem to be somewhat more satisfied when they work. Husbands again show much less discord with the housewife-type allocation scheme.

Dissatisfaction with household responsibilities for lower income women stays at about the same level (averaging about 30 percent in each subsample) across family life-cycle categories. But there are clear differences between working-wife and housewife families. Low-income housewives are more dissatisfied than their working counterparts in the prechild and young child stages, but more satisfied in the later stages. Their husbands' feeling are parallel, except in the prechild stage. Higher-income wives are generally more satisfied with the housework allocation scheme when they work, except in the young child stage, where there is equally high dissatisfaction in both types of families. The husbands are, in general, much

TABLE 5.3 Specific Role Dissatisfaction by Wife's Work Status in Various Family Life-Cycle and Income Situations

Preference-Role	Prechild		Youngest less than 6		Youngest 6+		Empty Nest	
	Low Inc.[3]	High Inc.[4]	Low Inc.	High Inc.	Low Inc.	High Inc.	Low Inc.	High Inc.
Discord:								
Wife's Preference[1]								
Housewife	64.3 (14)	42.9 (7)	33.8 (68)	33.3 (81)	22.5 (40)	22.4 (49)	39.3 (28)	20.0 (25)
Working Wife	42.9 (7)	11.1 (9)	33.3 (18)	35.4 (31)	30.0 (10)	33.3 (54)	42.9 (7)	12.5 (24)
Husband's Preference[1]								
Housewife	35.7 (14)	16.7 (15)	16.2 (68)	11.5 (78)	10.3 (39)	14.9 (47)	7.7 (26)	12.5 (24)
Working Wife	28.6 (7)	0.0 (6)	50.0 (16)	42.9 (28)	60.0 (10)	46.0 (50)	83.3 (6)	38.1 (21)
Chore Dissatisfaction:								
Wife[1]								
Housewife	35.7 (14)	0.0 (7)	33.8 (68)	33.8 (80)	31.6 (38)	28.6 (49)	25.0 (28)	16.0 (25)
Working Wife	28.6 (7)	25.0 (8)	22.2 (18)	32.3 (31)	40.0 (10)	32.7 (53)	42.9 (7)	32.0 (25)
Husband[2]								
Housewife	0.0 (6)	25.0 (4)	11.7 (60)	10.9 (55)	18.8 (16)	8.1 (37)	0.0 (24)	14.3 (28)
Working Wife	5.9 (17)	5.9 (17)	5.0 (20)	9.7 (31)	33.3 (15)	8.0 (50)	15.4 (13)	16.7 (30)

1. Female respondents.
2. Male respondents.
3. Family income under $12,000 per year.
4. Family income over $12,000 per year.

more satisfied with housework allocation than their wives and, where sample size is large enough to be reliable, show little difference by type of family task allocation scheme.

In general, wife's work status is most salient to her own preference-role discord in the prechild stage. For lower-income women, the wife's absence from the labor force is "unexcused" and helps keep the family at an uncomfortably low income level. Except for the prechild, lower-income family, the wife's dissatisfaction with the allocation of household chores is affected by her work status when no children are present (she is more likely to be dissatisfied if she works). The saliency of her work status is not as great when children are present, though there is a tendency for the working wife to be more dissatisfied with household chore allocation when children are older, and for the housewife to be more dissatisfied with the allocation of household chores when young children are present.

The husband's preference-role discord as it relates to his wife's work status tends to be greater for lower-income families, particularly if the wife works. For both income groups, the working wife is more likely to be in a position opposed to her husband's wishes than is the housewife in every life-cycle stage except prechild. This is especially the case when children are present, but even in the empty nest stage it is true, though it is possible that this is a generation of cohort effect rather than a result of the absence of children, since couples in this older age group tend to be more conservative.

These results show first that it is not role structure *alone* that determines satisfaction with roles in the family, but also the external and internal conditions under which that structure exists. When children are not present, and particularly before they arrive, the wife tends to be happiest with her role when she works, regardless of family income. In the prechild stage, the husband feels likewise. He tends to have less dissatisfaction in the empty nest stage, however, when she stays home. When children are present, work-role satisfaction is about the same for the wife whether or not she works outside the home, though the husband—particularly the lower-family-income husband—shows strong dissatisfaction when she works.

There seem, then, to be conflicting costs and benefits for the wife's outside work role when children are present. Each choice has its satisfactions—outside work satisfactions or material ones—and its negative aspects—time overload or the feeling of being trapped in the home. From the husband's standpoint, the wife's place typically is seen as being in the home when children are present. It is, of course, impossible with the present data to do anything but suggest cause-and-effect relationships. There is clearly some selection, such that women who work when children are present are those most committed to their jobs, either for economic or personal satisfaction reasons. However, as Table 5.3 shows, the overall level of preference-role discord varies by family circumstance (regardless of wife's work status), and these changes are at least partly the result of a lack of fit between family needs, personal needs, and chosen role structure. Analyses in Chapters 2 and 4 showed that the choice of work-housework allocation scheme—especially wife's work status—is partly rational: it can be partially explained as an attempt to maximize profits in the face of social and economic contingencies. Nevertheless, much dissatisfaction still exists.

We turn next to the effect of the wife's choice of housewife or worker role on the nature of the marital bond itself. As used here, Affection and Instrumentality are two distinct continuums, rather than polar types. In addition, they are directional, so that husband and wife may differ to the extent that one is bound—affectionally or instrumentally—to the other. For each life-cycle/income-level subsample, Affection and Instrumentality scores were computed for the housewife and working-wife families. The responses of husband and wife are given separately.

Regardless of family income, the wife receives more affection from her husband when she works *if* no children are present (see Table 5.4). Working wives also receive more affection in the case where the family has a low income and where older

TABLE 5.4 Type of Marital Bond by Wife's Work Status in Various Family Life-Cycle and Income Situations

	Prechild		Youngest less than 6		Youngest 6+		Empty Nest	
	Low Inc.[3]	High Inc.[4]	Low Inc.	High Inc.	Low Inc.	High Inc.	Low Inc.	High Inc.
Affectional Bond[1]								
Housewife	3.14 (14)	2.57 (7)	3.29 (69)	3.29 (82)	3.08 (40)	3.31 (49)	2.86 (28)	3.04 (25)
Working Wife	3.71 (7)	2.78 (9)	2.72 (18)	2.93 (31)	3.20 (31)	2.93 (55)	3.57 (7)	3.44 (25)
Affectional Bond[2]								
Housewife	3.83 (6)	3.75 (4)	3.27 (60)	3.22 (55)	3.44 (16)	3.14 (37)	3.42 (24)	3.34 (29)
Working Wife	3.82 (17)	3.28 (18)	3.25 (20)	3.03 (31)	3.00 (15)	3.18 (50)	3.54 (13)	3.19 (31)
Instrumental Bond[1]								
Housewife	2.43 (14)	2.43 (7)	2.55 (69)	2.56 (82)	2.83 (40)	2.84 (49)	3.07 (28)	2.92 (25)
Working Wife	2.71 (7)	2.33 (9)	2.33 (18)	2.23 (31)	2.80 (10)	2.78 (55)	2.43 (7)	3.12 (25)
Instrumental Bond[2]								
Housewife	2.17 (6)	3.75 (4)	2.17 (60)	2.69 (55)	2.81 (16)	2.65 (37)	3.29 (24)	2.83 (29)
Working Wife	3.71 (17)	2.78 (18)	2.90 (20)	2.68 (31)	2.80 (15)	2.78 (50)	3.31 (13)	3.03 (31)

1. Female respondents.
2. Male respondents.
3. Family income under $12,000 per year.
4. Family income over $12,000 per year.

children are present. (Her income in this case may be so essential to family well-being that the husband "rewards" her for it.) Otherwise, whenever children are living at home, the wife receives more affection if she stays out of the labor force.

In general, the husband is more likely to receive affection from his wife when she stays out of the labor force. In only one case (empty nest, low family income) is the opposite true. In the other cases, either it makes no substantial difference (3 subsamples) whether or not the wife works, or the husband receives more affection from his wife if she is not working (4 subsamples).

There seems to be no clear pattern of wife's perception of her husband's instrumentality, except that she generally sees him as more instrumental if she does not work. This is undoubtedly a *cause* of her not working, however, in addition to being an effect; if her husband is a good provider, she is less likely to enter the work force.

The husband sees his wife as more instrumental when she works in the prechild and young family stages for the low-income group, and in the older family and empty nest stages for the high-income group. In only one case is the housewife viewed as more instrumental than the working wife (prechild, high-income group), but in this case the small cell size ($N = 4$) makes any conclusions unwarranted.

The evidence on instrumentality is thus mixed, and the casual direction often difficult to interpret as it is related to the wife's work status. The affectional bond is somewhat clearer: The wife receives affection from her husband if she works when children are not present, and if she stays home when children are present. She tends to give affection more when she stays out of the labor force, probably as a function of the heavy time-energy load she must sustain when she works.

AFFECTION-INSTRUMENTALITY AND OTHER MEASURES OF THE MARRIAGE RELATIONSHIP

Before moving to an analysis of global marital quality measures, it will be useful to discuss the conceptual and empirical link between these and the nature of the marital bond. Affection and Instrumentality variables are in one sense measures of the "worth" of a spouse to his or her mate and thus specify "reasons for staying together." Most measures of marital quality are more general indicators of the state of the relationship between husband and wife. Though we expect bond strength to be related to the perceived quality of the marital relationship, it is a different kind of measure, and the relationship between the strength of different bond types and the quality of the relationship can usefully be treated as an empirical question and should shed light on the nature of each.

The AI scale is a composite of the Affection and Instrumentality scales, and its development and rationale have already been described. It has four categories made up of the two dichotomized scales. Table 5.5 demonstrates how four global and two behavioral measures of marital quality are related to the AI scale. The behavioral measures are the Positive and Negative Marital Scales (described above), and the four global measures are Getting Along Well with Souse, Marital Closeness, Marital Happiness, and Wanting to Stay Married.

The AI scale is significantly related to each of the six marital quality measures (all at the .001 level). The eta's vary in strength, however, with Marital Closeness showing the strongest relationship and Negative Marital Relations the weakest. Comparing the discordant categories on the AI scales (Affectional Only and Instrumental Only), it is clear that affection rather than instrumentality is the most important determinant of overall marital quality. This finding is supported by other studies in the literature (Lewis and Spanier, 1979). For marital closeness, marital happiness, and wanting to stay married, a strong affectional bond alone brings approximately the same quality to the relationship as do both the affectional and instrumental bonds combined. Only for "getting along well" and the behavioral measures does there seem to be an additive effect of the two types of bonds.

Instrumental ties seem to be associated with better day-to-day relations. There are fewer disagreements, more positive sharing activities, and in general spouses just get along better.

TABLE 5.5 Affection-Instrumentality and the Marital Quality Variables

		Affection-Instrumentality (AI)					
		Both	Affectional Only	Instrumental Only	Neither	eta^2 –	sig.
Positive Marital	M[1]	.48	.20	.11	-.34	14.1	.001
Relations	F[1]	.53	.38	-.02	-.42	17.8	.001
Negative Marital	M	-.07	.14	.19	.33	2.3	.02
Relations	F	-.13	.01	.49	.22	3.5	.001
Want to Stay	M	.94	.95	.84	.82	3.9	.001
Married (% very)	F	.99	.99	.91	.85	6.3	.001
Marital Happiness	M	.74	.71	.56	.50	5.0	.001
(% very)	F	.78	.78	.36	.49	9.8	.001
Marital Closeness	M	.84	.84	.48	.60	8.7	.001
(% very)	F	.93	.81	.55	.49	16.0	.001
Get along well	M	.80	.72	.60	.56	4.8	.001
(% very)	F	.90	.74	.56	.51	11.3	.001

1. Male respondents (wife's performance).
2. Female respondents (husband's performance).

But the affectional bond is even more important. Indeed, for more general measures of closeness, happiness, and wanting to stay married, affection produces as strong a relationship as the two scales combined. This fact casts light on the previous discussion regarding affection and instrumental bonds and how work-housework allocation schemes affect them in different circumstances. It also casts light on the next analysis of global measures of quality, in that the explanation for the effect of a work allocation scheme on these commonly used variables is likely to lie at least partly in its effect on the affectional bond.

THE BEHAVIORAL MEASURES

The global marital quality variables are of two types—behavioral and general. The behavioral are measures of the extent of positive and negative interactions between husband and wife, with the positive measured by the frequency with which certain pleasant activities are shared, and the negative by the number of different areas in which the husband and wife frequently disagree.

These Positive and Negative Relations Scales are broken down by wife's work status for each of the eight family circumstance subsamples. Response of husband and wife are presented separately. Unlike the Affection and Instrumentality variables, which are by definition directional (that is, spouse-specific), and the global measures, which tap general affect toward the marriage and are also therefore likely to be spouse-specific, the behavioral measures should in principle be relatively similar for husband and wife, even though the sample is not of couples.

A look at Table 5.6, however, demonstrates that this expected similarity does not appear. A close look at the items involved, such as "been affectionate toward each other" and "did something the other particularly appreciated," indicates that there may not only be what might be called "definitional" distortion of perception (What does "affectionate"mean?), but other kinds as well. For these two items particularly, the behavior in question has a directional quality (one gives and one receives), and either spouse may be more likely to perceive a "sharing" when he or she is on the receiving end. For example, the wife thinks her marriage is more characterized by positive interaction when she works, except for the upper-income wife with children present. In the previous section we saw that wives *receive* more affection when they work if children are not present but, with certain exceptions, give more when they don't. The positive interaction variable, therefore, tends to be strongly related to the *reception* of affection, and this seems to be where the perceptual distortion lies. Thus, the husband sees more positive interaction in most situations when the wife does *not* work outside the home.

When it comes to disagreements between husband and wife, we see that the evidence is fairly consistent that working wives seem to create more problem areas and have more sources of disagreement with their husbands than do housewives. The positive dimension of the relationship, however, seems to be subject to substantial perceptive distortion. The wife thinks her marriage is more positive in this regard when she works because she receives more affection from her husband, except in the case of the upper-income wife, who sees the housewife role as better when children are present. The working wife from a lower-income family has more positive interaction with her husband even when children are present, probably because her income contribution is so vital to the family's viability that her husband rewards her for it.

In general, then, an outside work role for the wife means more intense interaction with her husband. There are generally more areas of disagreement, but when children are not present, from the wife's viewpoint there is more positive interaction as well.

GENERAL MEASURES

Two general measures—Marital Happiness and Martial Closeness—were chosen for the detailed analysis. Marital happiness is perhaps the most widely used and is certainly the most general measure of affect toward the marital relationship. Marital

TABLE 5.6 Marriage Quality Measures by Wife's Work Status in Various Family Life-Cycle and Income Situations

	Family Life Cycle/Composition							
	Prechild		Youngest less than 6		Youngest 6+		Empty Nest	
	Low Inc.[3]	High Inc.[4]	Low Inc.	High Inc.	Low Inc.	High Inc.	Low Inc.	High Inc.
Positive Relations[5]								
Wife[1]								
Housewife	.10 (14)	-.07 (7)	-.10 (69)	.25 (82)	-.01 (40)	.11 (49)	-.18 (28)	.02 (25)
Working Wife	.50 (7)	.49 (9)	.18 (18)	-.55 (31)	.13 (10)	-.13 (55)	.05 (7)	.52 (25)
Husband[2]								
Housewife	.71 (6)	.45 (4)	.02 (60)	.22 (55)	-.05 (16)	.03 (37)	.08 (24)	.43 (29)
Working Wife	.56 (17)	.40 (18)	.13 (20)	.02 (31)	-.43 (15)	-.06 (50)	-.38 (13)	-.11 (31)
Negative Relations[5]								
Wife[1]								
Housewife	.52 (14)	.16 (7)	.38 (69)	.31 (82)	.09 (40)	-.19 (49)	-.26 (28)	-.65 (25)
Working Wife	.88 (7)	.39 (9)	.39 (18)	.25 (31)	.34 (10)	-.19 (55)	.52 (7)	-.32 (25)
Husband[2]								
Housewife	.48 (6)	.34 (4)	.55 (60)	.30 (55)	.29 (16)	-.01 (37)	-.47 (24)	-.54 (29)
Working Wife	.66 (17)	.39 (18)	.64 (20)	.35 (31)	.09 (15)	.09 (50)	-.14 (13)	-.46 (31)

Marital Happiness[6]

Wife[1]								
Housewife	79 (14)	57 (7)	61 (69)	68 (82)	65 (40)	63 (49)	61 (28)	68 (25)
Working Wife	100 (7)	56 (19)	56 (18)	48 (31)	60 (10)	60 (55)	71 (7)	72 (25)
Husband[2]								
Housewife	83 (6)	75 (4)	55 (60)	64 (55)	69 (16)	51 (37)	75 (24)	79 (29)
Working Wife	82 (17)	78 (18)	50 (20)	48 (31)	40 (15)	52 (50)	69 (13)	77 (31)

Marital Closeness[7]

Wife[1]								
Housewife	86 (6)	71 (4)	67 (69)	70 (82)	65 (40)	71 (49)	64 (28)	68 (25)
Working Wife	100 (17)	78 (18)	56 (18)	55 (31)	70 (10)	69 (55)	100 (7)	76 (25)
Husband[2]								
Housewife	83 (6)	75 (4)	73 (60)	76 (55)	75 (16)	78 (37)	79 (24)	79 (29)
Working Wife	71 (17)	83 (18)	60 (20)	61 (31)	60 (15)	55 (50)	100 (13)	81 (31)

1. Female respondents.
2. Male respondents.
3. Family income under $12,000 per year.
4. Family income over $12,000 per year.
5. In standard score form.
6. Percentage very happy.
7. Percentage very close.

[147]

closeness is the best measure of the overall strength of the relationship. Earlier comparisons with the AI scale (see Table 5.5) demonstrated that it is primarily a function of the affectional dimension of marriage. "Wanting to Stay Married," at first thought to be the ideal measure of the probability of future dissolution, shows so little variance that it is not used here.

As with the behavioral and Affection-Instrumentality variables, marital closeness and happiness are broken down by wife's work status for each of the eight family circumstance subsamples. In general, happiness and closeness seem to show similar patterns. Low-income husbands are happier with their marriages and feel closer to their wives when the wife stays home, except in the empty nest period, when they feel closer in the working-wife case. If we concentrate on those comparisons where the difference between housewife and working-wife families is 5 percent or more, high-income males and both lower- and upper-income wives all show similar patterns: They are happier and feel closer when the wife works if there are no children present, and are happier and feel closer when she does *not* work if children are present.

SUMMARY

No one work allocation scheme is inherently better or worse for a given family. As the foregoing analyses make clear, different schemes are better in different circumstances.

Prechild/Low Family Income

Marriages seem to be more viable when the wife works. This is certainly true of the wife's feelings, though less true of the husband's, since he generally gets less affection when his wife works. The importance of the wife's income contribution—her instrumental value—makes it easier for him to put up with her working, however.

Prechild/Middle to High Family Income

Working-wife marriages still have the edge, though the situation is not as clear cut. The working wife gets more affection from her husband, but the instrumental bonds now run in the opposite direction. In general, though, working wife arrangements are characterized by close relationships and are still preferred by both partners.

Young Children at Home/Low Fmaily Income

Housewife families seem to be more viable. The housewife is more bound to her husband in terms of both affection and instrumentality, and the marriage is closer and happier. There seems to be more positive interaction in working-wife families, however, and the wife is more valuable to the husband in terms of his nonemotional needs.

Young Children at Home/Moderate to High Family Income

Housewife families are clearly more viable. For every measure of marital quality, there is either no clear pattern or the housewife families are clearly superior.

Older Children at Home/Low Family Income

Housewife families again seem to be more viable, but the importance of extra income somewhat weakens the relationship. The working wife receives more affection from her husband, perceives more positive interaction, and sees the marriage as closer (though not as happy). The housewife arrangement is clearly preferred by both spouses, however.

Older Children at Home/Moderate to High Family Income

The income level seems to make only a small difference in this life-cycle category. The wife's potential income is slightly less vital to the family's survival, so that the negative aspects of working while there are children at home seem to predominate.

Empty Nest/Low Family Income

Though the housewife families are favored in terms of preference-role discord, working-wife families tend to be closer.

Empty nest working-wife families seem to be more active here; there are more disagreements over a variety of issues, but more affection as well. Perhaps for this reason working-wife families in this category may be viewed as more viable.

Empty Nest/Moderate to High Family Income

There is a pronounced sex split in this category. Working wives see their marriages as more positive than do housewives, though there tend to be more disagreements. Husbands of working wives seem linked to them instrumentally, but see themselves as receiving fewer emotional returns than husbands of housewives.

In general terms, working-wife marriages seem more viable when children are not present. There seems to be more pressure on husbands than on wives, however, since the directionality of the affection bond seems to shift in her favor when she works. The work-housework allocation scheme therefore tends to affect other, more subtle roles. The working-wife family has an especially clear advantage when the wife's income is valuable to the family's financial solvency.

When children are present, the lesson seems to be that it is better if the wife stays home, particularly if her income is not important to the family's economic position. As we saw in Chapter 4, the impact on time and energy load is heavy, particularly on the working wife, when children are present. The impact on the husband is shown not so much in terms of his time as in loss of affection and the need to consume poorer-quality home goods. But the fact that the husband does not substantially change his participation in housework tasks with the advent of children means that working women with children undergo much more time and energy stress than their nonworking counterparts. Of course, these are only gross estimates. Many wives require the personal satisfaction of a career for a happy marriage. Yet the sacrifices are clearly greater when children are present.

In a general way, behavioral responses (see Chapters 2 and 4) to socioeconomic contingencies seem to be grossly rational, in that those families who do not fit the patterns (such as housewife families when children are not present, or working-wife families when they are present) seem somewhat less viable than families that "follow the crowd." But it must be said that the differences are not great, and that there seem to be many successful work-housework arrangements for any given set of socioeconomic contingencies.

NOTES

1. For a detailed review of the marital happiness and stability literature, see Hicks and Platt (1970), to whose analysis the following summary is much indebted. For a more recent if more narrowly focused review, see Gove and Peterson (1980).

2. A few husbands of nonworking wives do report that their wives are very good at "earning a good living," since some housewives are seen as only temporarily unemployed. But the instrumentality score is still downwardly biased for those women who have never worked. The problem here is not methodological, however, but theoretical. If we leave the choice, "earning a good living," out for housewives and standardize scores, we bias housewives upward relative to working wives, since working wives can be very good *both* at home and on the job and still have the same scores as housewives who are only good housewives. It was decided therefore to leave "earning a good living" as a possible choice for housewives, since working wives who are good both at home and on the job *should* receive higher scores than housewives who are simply good housewives.

3. We eliminated "entertained friends in your home," since one's living conditions might prevent one from inviting friends over. We eliminated "taking a drive or a walk for pleasure," since cars involve money, and walking in certain neighborhoods is a dangerous practice.

6

Summary and Conclusion

We have attempted to draw the outlines of a theory of family work-housework role allocation by drawing together theories and assumptions in economics and sociology, and to refine the theory empirically with data from a recent national sample. The welding of the economic and the sociological approach to the family can be accomplished primarily by stripping away certain assumptions of the structural-functionalist school of family sociology and by relaxing certain utility-maximizing assumptions in the theories of labor supply and the value of time in economics. Such a combination of approaches develops the image of a family acting at least partly as a utility-maximizing unit in its social and economic environment, and identifies those key characteristics of the family and its members that should determine its mode of adaptation to its environment. Yet we assume that the adaptation will be imperfect—that is, that particularly in times of rapid social change, many families will not evolve the best work-housework role structure, and under certain circumstances, the family may face only an array of bad choices. Thus, the viability of a particular mode of adaptation can and must be treated as an empirical question.

The theory is *family* functional rather than individual or societal functional. It takes from economics the idea that the family is not a closed system of interacting personalities, but exists in relation to the marketplace of goods and labor and must function in that system to survive. Sociology adds that it exists also in a sociocultural environment. It borrows from economics the idea that the family can usefully be approached as a utility-maximizing unit, and from sociology the notion that it is reasonable to attempt to measure utility—as complex as that problem may be—rather than use the concept as a tautological assumption. Such an approach has the potential of being simultaneously theoretically sound, empirically based, and prescriptive; in other words, relevant to individual families facing choices in the real world.

In American society at present, the key response of the family to its economic environment seems to be the choice of the wife's work role. Our analysis confirms those of other researchers in that husband's wage, wife's potential wage, and the demand for child care in the home are the three most important determinants of the wife's choice of role.

Other factors show some influence. Attitudes held by the wife toward the "proper" role of women have some impact on whether or not she enters the labor force, whereas the ideology of her husband has little impact. Rather than general endorsements of principles, specific opinions concerning proper behavior have the primary impact.

The key life-style decision involved in the choice of wife's work role thus seems to be made primarily in response to objective economic factors. Characteristics of the husband and wife that impact on her choice of work role are those most closely tied to the family's economic viability. These characteristics are not always tied to the external system in a simple linear way. The evidence, for example, shows that it is the possession of diplomas rather than education per se that increases the wife's labor market value to her family.

Though her choice of work role can be partly explained by her potential contribution to family utility—particularly financial—the wife makes the choice on the basis of personal satisfaction as well. The wife's perception of her husband's preferences also has an impact on her behavior. Indeed, it appears to function as the "voice of family utility." But her choice is also based on other factors. Though her preference and behavior often agree with her husband's preference (and the purely economic needs of her family), when there is disagreement, her own preference tends to override that of her husband.

Once the choice is made, there is always a degree of regret for what has been lost. Particularly when resources are low, every choice involves dissatisfactions. The mother who does not work because children are present may be foregoing income that could increase the family's standard of living or enhance her children's chances for a good education. The mother who does work may fear that her children are not receiving the care they need.

Given the choice of wife's work role, household tasks must also be allocated. We found that it is important that the time spent on housework (that is, the *volume* of activity) be considered separately from the *allocation of responsibility* for housework. In general, the time the husband spends on housework does not seem to vary by much. The volume of housework is primarily a function of the wife's work status and the presence and number of children. Responsibility allocation however, seems to be primarily a function of variables that represent access to economic and social resources, though not always in expected ways. Husband's resources seem to show primarily an ideology effect rather than a power or value-of-time effect; the more educated he is, the more he pitches in with the housework. Wife's resources seem to have a positive effect on the fairness of responsibility allocation—especially for working wives—but the effect is weak.

The family's work-housework role structure, then, is a complex response to its social and economic environment. The choice of a work role for the wife is primarily a response to the real and potential wage rates of the family members, and to the demand for housework and home goods in general that is created by children. The allocation of responsibility for housework is, above all, highly wife-skewed no matter what circumstances the family faces. Within this traditional and deeply engrained allocation system, there is relatively minor variation in responsibility. Variation is to be found primarily in the hours of housework performed by the wife, and there appears to be a marked degree of flexibility in housework time, so that through greater efficiency in use of time, acceptance of poorer-quality home goods, and employment of hired help or labor-saving devices, a family can drastically alter the total time required for housework. Shifts in the social and economic environment occasion only minor alterations in the housework time allocation system because of the husband's refusal to participate in housework beyond a certain level. Such shifts do, however, occasion sharp changes in the way housework is performed by the wife and, to a much lesser extent, the way responsibility for various tasks is allocated.

The work-housework role allocation structure, then, is only partly a rational adaptation to economic circumstances. The traditional structure, which opposes the work role for the wife and even more so the mother, seems to be crumbling—the percentage of working wives has been increasing about 1 percent per year since the early 1960s (Hayghe, 1976), but traditions concerning housework seem to die much harder, and there seems to be a lag at present between role allocation in the two arenas.

Having supported and, to some extent, expanded on the notion that the family's work-housework role allocation structure is its imperfect attempt to maximize utility in its social and economic environment, we have undertaken to examine the notion of family utility. Following from the arguments of the first chapter, it appeared possible to relate the notion of utility-maximization to the functionalists' notion of the viability of the family. We expect that the success of families' structural adaptations to socioeconomic contingencies will have ramifications for the viability of the family unit itself, and indeed, indicators of viability might be taken as a measure of successful adaptation.

Viability rests on many factors, and the approach we settled on does not attempt to choose a single measure of a successful, viable marriage. Instead, a variety of measures were chosen tapping various dimensions of the relationship. Specifically, we studied the type of marital bond, the frequency and quality of shared behavior that characterized the relationship, and the general feelings toward the relationship of husband and wife. Even with this approach, it became clear that spouses generally overemphasize the positive nature of their marriages. It is difficult with this kind of survey to detect deep-seated problems in marriages.

In addition to some rather striking evidence of perceptive distortion, it was found that there was a good deal of variation in the quality and viability of marital relationships. Our analyses focused on the choice of wife's work role and the ramifications for marital quality in different family income and life-cycle situations. As expected, we found that it is not primarily the work allocation system per se that determines marital viability, but rather its appropriateness given the circumstances in which the family finds itself.

Basically, the presence of children seems to create problems that a working-wife role allocation system may have more difficulty solving than a housewife system. It seems to be better for all concerned when the wife works if no children are present. Relative to this particular conclusion, however, at least three caveats are in order.

First, the selection of causal direction is always tricky when human actors are involved, and seems particularly problematic here. We saw the problem when discussing sex-role attitudes among wives and their choice of the working role. Might not the experience of working at a job influence one's attitude as much as one's attitude influencing the decision to take a job? Some evidence suggests that this might be the case (Molm, 1978). In the case under discussion here, perhaps wives in less viable marriages choose to work even when children are present because they require a source of satisfaction outside the home.

Second, we have seen clearly that the heavy demand for housework created by children falls primarily on the wife. Perhaps it is not the fact that the wife works, but rather the fact that she receives an uncompensated housework burden with the advent of children that makes working-wife marriages with children present less successful. Two lessons present themselves here: first, the importance of looking at the entire work-housework system, and second, the fact that tradition or culture must be included as part of the socioeconomic contingencies to which the family adapts.

Third, it is important to point out that the level of resources available to a family and the demand for those resources created by the presence of children seem to have an effect on marital quality, independent of the role structure that is created to meet those circumstances. As we pointed out earlier, in some situations families face only an array of bad choices. A childless couple where the husband makes a substantial income can easily adapt to a situation in which the wife works or in which she does not. If she works, it is a relatively simple matter to eat out more often or hire help to take up the slack. If she does not work, her foregone income will not be sorely missed. But when the husband's income is low and there are many children, there is a great demand for both an additional income and for the presence of the wife at home during the day. In this case, *any* work-housework role allocation system will create difficulties for the relationship.

This type of analysis has its limitations. An empirical study of such complex questions inevitably requires some simplification of concepts and variables. For example, we know from our own day-to-day experience that important family decisions such as the wife's entry into the labor force are often the outcome of very complex bargaining processes. These processes include elements of power, some of which flows from authority relationships, as well as elements of love and trust, and of ignorance and deceit—both of oneself and of others. Only through an in-depth, detailed study of these processes can we gain a sense of family, a gut-level sense of the way these decisions are made. The more global, statistical approach used here forces us to throw many of these processes into the time-worn black box.

Future research on work-housework role allocation cannot afford to ignore either of two facts. First, the structure is not evolved in a vacuum—that is, the choice of allocation structure is not made randomly, nor in response only to the role expectations of the society or of the sex-role ideology of husband and wife. These factors have some impact, but they are minor compared to economic circumstances, especially regarding wife's work role. Since the structure evolves in reaction to objective circumstances—not all of which the family can control—and since these circumstances themselves have an impact on personal happiness and the quality of relationships, the structure must be judged in terms of its *adaptive* success relative to particular circumstances rather than per se.

Second, the utility of any structural adaptation to circumstances must always be treated as an empirical question. Nonutilitarian choices are not statistical rubbish to be shoved aside or ignored; they are vital social data, since they serve to define those ways of structuring marital life which are successful.

Future research must focus on identifying those sets of circumstances that make one type of work-housework role allocation more successful than another. This is not an easy task, since, as we have seen, it is difficult to draw samples of sufficient size so that families in a narrowly defined set of social and economic circumstances can be studied. Samples might best be drawn from a narrow segment of the population—for example, nuclear families with children under 3 years old—and then divided into circumstance groups based on income and other key economic variables. A number of such studies over a period of time would allow us to speak with more authority about the circumstances that are most important in determining whether a particular mode of work-housework role allocation is successful. It would also allow us to separate out aspects of the allocation system for study other than wife's work status, especially the allocation of housework as it relates to family utility. Such research, by focusing on key areas of family decision making and by carefully studying the ramifications of various role allocation decisions on the quality of family life, should aim to produce something all too rare in academic sociology and economics: a prescriptive theory that is *empirically* rather than *ideologically* based.

Bibliography

ANDREWS, F. M., T. N. MORGAN, and T. A. SONQUIST (1973) Multiple Classification Analysis. Ann Arbor: University of Michigan, Institute for Social Research.

ARMEN, A. (1969) Exchange and Production: Theory in Use. Belmont, CA: Wadsworth.

BARTH, E. and W. WATSON (1967) "Social stratification and the family in mass society." Social Forces 45: 392-402.

BECKER, G. S. (1974) "A theory of marriage: part III." Journal of Political Economy 82 (March/April).

———(1973) "A theory of marriage: part I." Journal of Political Economy 81 (July/August).

———(1965) "A theory of the allocation of time." Economic Journal 75: 493-517.

BELL, N. W. and E. F. VOGEL (1960) "Toward a framework for functional analysis of family behavior," in N. W. Bell and E. F. Vogel (eds.) A Modern Introduction to the Family. New York: Free Press.

BERK, R. and S. BERK (1979) Labor and Leisure in the Home. Beverly Hills, CA: Sage.

BLOOD, R. O. (1963) "The husband-wife relationship," in F. I. Nye and L. Hoffman (eds.) The Employed Mother in America. Chicago: Rand McNally.

———and R. HAMBLIN (1958) "The effect of the wife's employment on the family power structure." Social Forces 36: 347-352.

———and D. M. WOLFE (1969) Husband and Wives: The Dynamics of Married Living. Glencoe, IL: Free Press.

BOWEN, W. G. and T. A. FINEGAN (1969) The Economics of Labor Force Participation. Princeton, NJ: Princeton University Press.

BURGESS, E. W. (1962) "The family: a unity of interacting personalities." The Family 7: 3-9.

———and L. S. CORTRELL (1939) Predicting Success or Failure in Marriage. Englewood Cliffs, NJ: Prentice-Hall.

BURGESS, E. W. and H. J. LOCKE (1945) The Family: From Institution to Companionship. New York: American Books.

BURGESS, E. W. and P. WALLIN (1953) Engagement and Marriage. Philadelphia: J. B. Lippincott.

BURR, W. R., R. HILL, F. I. NYE, and I. L. REIS [eds.] (1979) "Introduction," in W. R. Burr et al. (eds.) Contemporary Theories About the Family: Research-Based Theories, Vol. I. New York: Free Press.

CAIN, G. G. (1966) Married Women in the Labor Force. Chicago:

CAMPBELL, A., P. E. CONVERSE, and W. L. ROGERS (1976) The Quality of American Life: Perceptions, Evaluations. New York: Russell Sage Foundation.

CAMPBELL, F. L. (1970) "Family in growth and variation in family role structure." Journal of Marriage and the Family 32: 45-53.

CHRISTENSEN, H. T. [ed.] (1964) Handbook of Marriage and the Family. Chicago: Rand McNally.

DOWDALL, J. A. (1974) "Structural and attitudinal factors associated with female labor force participation." Social Science Quarterly 55: 121-130.

FARKAS, G. (1975) "Education, wage rates, and the division of labor between husband and wife." Presented at the annual meetings of the American Sociological Association, August.

FOGARTY, M. P., R. RAPOPORT, and R. N. RAPOPORT (1971) Career, Sex, and Family. London: Allen & Unwin.

GANS, H. (1962) The Urban Villagers. New York: Free Press.

GOVE, W. and C. PETERSON (1980) "An update of the literature on personal and marital adjustment: the effect of children and the employment of wives." Marriage and Family Review 3 (Fall/Winter): 63-69.

GOVE, W. and M. HUGHES (1980) "Sex differences in physical illness and how medical sociologists view illness behavior." American Sociological Review 45: 514-522.

———and O. GALLE (1983) Overcrowding in the Home: Social and Structural Determinants of its Effects. New York: Academic.

GRAMM, W. L. (1975) "Household utility maximization and the working wife." American Economic Review 65: 90-100.

GREENFIELD, S. M. (1966) English Rustics in Black Skin. New Haven, CT: College & University Press.

GRONAU, R. (1977) "Leisure, home production and work." Journal of Political Economy (December): 1099-1123.

———(1976) "The allocation of time of Israeli women." Journal of Political Economy (August): 5201-5220.

———(1973) "The intrafamily allocation of time: the value of housewives' time." American Economic Review 63: 635-651.

GURIN, G., J. VEROFF, and S. FELD (1960) Americans View Their Mental Health. New York: Basic Books.

HALLER, M. and L. ROSENMAYER (1971) "The pluridimensionality of work commitment." Human Relations 24: 501-518.

HAUG, M. R. (1973) "Social class measurement and women's occupational roles." Social Forces 52: 86-98.

HAYGHE, H. (1976) "Families and the rise of working wives—an overview." Monthly Labor Review 99: 12-19.

———(1974) "Marital and family characteristics of the labor force in March 1973." Monthly Labor Review 97: 21-27.

HEATH, A. (1976) Rational Choice and Social Exchange: A Critique of Exchange Theory. Cambridge, Eng.: Cambridge University Press.

HEDGES, J. N. and J. K. BARNEETT (1972) "Working women and the division of household tasks." Monthly Labor Review 95: 9-14.

HEER, D. M. (1963) "The measurement and bases of family power: an overview." Marriage and Family Living 25: 133-139.

HESSELBART, S. (1976) "Does charity begin at home? Attitudes toward women, household tasks, and household decision-making." Presented at the annual meetings of the American Sociological Association, August.

HICKS, M. and M. PLATT (1970) "Marital happiness and stability: a review of research in the sixties." Journal of Marriage and the Family 32: 553-574.

HILL, R. and D. A. HANSEN (1960) "The identification of conceptual frameworks utilized in family study." Marriage and Family Living 22: 299-311.

HODGE, R., P. SIEGLE, and P. ROSSI (1964) "Occupation prestige in the United States." American Journal of Sociology 70: 286-302.

HOFFMAN, L. W. (1974) "Effects on child," in L. W. Hoffman and F. I. Nye (eds.) Working Mothers. San Francisco: Jossey-Bass.

———(1963) "The decision to work," in F. I. Nye and L. W. Hoffman (eds.) The Employed Mother in America. Chicago: Rand McNally.

———(1960) "Effect of the employment of mothers on parental power relations and the division of household tasks." Marriage and Family Living 22: 27-35.

KAHNE, H. and A. KOHEN (1975) "Economic perspectives on the roles of women in the American economy." Journal of Economic Literature 13: 1249-1292.

KANTOR, D. and W. LEHR (1975) Inside the Family. New York: Harper & Row.

KOMAROVSKY, M. (1962) Blue Collar Marriage. New York: Random House.

LEIBENSTEIN, H. (1976) Beyond Economic Man. Cambridge, MA: Harvard University Press.

LEIBOWITZ, A. (1975) "Women's work in the home," in C. B. Lloyd (ed.) Sex, Discrimination and the Division of Labor. New York: Columbia University Press.

LEWIS, R. A. and G. B. SPANIER (1979) "Theorizing about the quality and stability of marriage," in W. R. Burr et al. (eds.) Contemporary Theories About the Family, Vol. I. New York: Free Press.

LIVELY, E. (1969) "Toward conceptual clarification: case of marital interaction." Journal of Marriage and the Family 31: 108-114.

LLOYD, C. B. (1975) "The division of labor between the sexes: a review," in C. B. Lloyd (ed.) Sex, Discrimination and the Division of Labor. New York: Columbia University Press.

LUCKEY, E. (1964) "Marital satisfaction and personality correlates of spouse." Journal of Marriage and the Family 26: 217-220.

MEISSNER, M., E. W. HUMPHRY, S. M. MEISS, and W. J. SCHEU (1975) "No exit for wives; sexual division of labor and the cumulation of household demands." Canadian Review of Sociology and Anthropology 12: 424-459.

MERTON, R. K. (1957) "Manifest and latent functions," in R. K. Merton, Theory and Social Structure. New York: Free Press.

MINCER, J. (1962) "Labor force participation of married women: a study of labor supply," in Aspects of Labor Economics. Princeton, NJ: National Bureau Committee for Economic Research.

MOLM, L. D. (1978) "Sex role attitudes and the employment of married women: the direction of casuality." Sociological Quarterly 19: 522-533.

MORGAN, J., I. SIRAGELDIN, and N. BAERWALDT (1966) Productive Americans: A Study of How Individuals Contribute to Economic Growth. Ann Arbor: University of Michigan.

NYE, F. I. [ed.] (1976) Role Structure and Analysis of the Family. Beverly Hills, CA: Sage.

————and V. GECAS (1976) "The role concept: review and delineation," in F. I. Nye (ed.) Role Structure and Analysis of the Family. Beverly Hills, CA: Sage.

NYE, F. I., J. CARLSON, and G. GARRETT (1970) "Family size, interaction, and stress." Journal of Marriage and the Family 32: 216-226.

OAKLEY, A. (1974) The Sociology of Housework. New York: Pantheon.

OPPENHEIMER, V. K. (1977) "The sociology of women's economic role in the family." American Sociological Review 42: 387-405.

ORDEN, S. R. and N. M. BRADBURN (1968) "Dimensions of marital happiness." American Journal of Sociology 74: 715-731.

PARSONS, T. (1949) Essays in Sociological Theory: Pure and Applied. New York: Free Press.

————(1943) "The kinship system of the contemporary United States." American Anthropologist 45: 22-38.

————and R. F. BALES (1955) Family, Socialization, and Interaction Process. New York: Free Press.

PHILLIBER, W. W. and D. V. HILLER (1978) "The implication of wife's occupational attainment for husband's class identification." Sociological Quarterly 19: 450-458.

PLECK, J. H. and J. NICHOLS (1977) "Work-family role system." Social Problems 24: 417-427.

POLOMA, M. M. (1970) "The myth of the egalitarian family: familial roles and the professionally employed wife." Presented at the annual meetings of the American Sociological Association.

————and T. N. GARLAND (1971) "The married professional woman: a study in the tolerance of domestication." Journal of Marriage and the Family 33: 531-540.

POWELL, K. S. (1961) "Maternal employment in relation to family life." Marriage and Family Living 23: 350-355.

RADCLIFFE-BROWN, A. R. (1935) "On the concept of function in social science." American Anthropologist 37: 394-402.

RAINWATER, L., R. P. COLEMAN, and G. HANDEL (1959) Workingman's Wife. Dobbs Ferry, NY: Oceana.

RAPOPORT, R. and R. N. RAPOPORT (1971) Dual-Career Families. Harmondsworth, Eng.: Penguin.

RITTER, K. V. and L. L. HARGENS (1975) "Occupational positions and class identification of married working women: a test of the asymmetry hypothesis." American Journal of Sociology 80: 934-948.

ROBINSON, J. (1977) How Americans Use Time. New York: Praeger.

ROLLINS, B. C. and K. L. CANNON (1974) "Marital satisfaction over the family life cycle: a reevaluation." Journal of Marriage and the Family 36: 271-282.

ROLLINS, B. C. and H. FELDMAN (1970) "Marital satisfaction over the family life cycle." Journal of Marriage and the Family 32: 20-28.

ROSENFIELD, C. and V. C. PERRELLA (1965) "Why women start and stop working: a study in mobility." Monthly Labor Review (September): 1077-1082.

ROSSI, P., W. A. SAMPSON, C. BOSE, G. PASSEL, and J. PASSEL (1974) "Measuring household standing." Social Science Research 3: 169-190.

SAFILIOS-ROTHSCHILD, C. (1970) "The study of family power structure: a review, 1900-1969." Journal of Marriage and the Family 32: 539-551.

SCANZONI, J. H. (1970) Opportunity and the Family. New York: Free Press.

SCHVANEVELDT, J.D. (1966) "The interactional framework in the study of the family," in F. I. Nye and F. M. Berardo (eds.) Emerging Conceptual Frameworks in Family Analysis. New York: Macmillan.

SLATER, P. E. (1961) "Parental role differentiation." American Journal of Sociology 67: 296-308.

SOBOL, M. G. (1974) "Commitment to work," in L. W. Hoffman and F. I. Nye (eds.) Working Mothers. San Francisco: Jossey-Bass.

———(1973) "Commitment to work," in F. I. Nye and L. W. Hoffman (eds.) The Employed Mother in America. Chicago: Rand McNally.

SPANIER, G. B., R. A. LEWIS, and C. L. COLE (1975) "Marital adjustment over the family life cycle: the issue of curveilinearity." Journal of Marriage and the Family 37: 263-275.

SWEET, J. (1973) Women in the Labor Force. New York: Academic.

SZALAI, A. (1975) "Women's time: women in the light of contemporary time-budget research." Futures (October).

———(1966) "Trends in comparative time-budget research." American Behavioral Scientist 9: 9.

———P. CONNERSE, P. FELDHEIM, E. SCHEUCH, and P. STONE [eds.] (1973) The Use of Time: Daily Activities of Urban and Suburban Populations in Twelve Countries. The Hague: Mouton.

VANEK, J. (1973) "Keeping busy: time spent in housework, United States, 1920-1970." Ph.D. dissertation, University of Michigan.

WALDMAN, E. and R. WHITMORE (1974) "Children of working mothers, March, 1973." Monthly Labor Review (May): 50-58.

WALKER, K. E. (1969) "Time spent in household by homemakers." Family Economic Review 3: 5-7.

———and W. H. GAUGER (1973) "Time and its dollar value in household work." Family Economic Review 7: 8-13.

———(1970) "Time spent by husbands in household work." Family Economic Review 4: 8-11.

WILENSKY, H. L. (1961) "The uneven distribution of leisure: the impact of economic growth on 'free time.'" Social Problems 9: 107-145.

WOLFE, D. M. (1959) "Power and authority in the family," in D. Cartwright (ed.) Studies in Social Power. Ann Arbor: University of Michigan.

About the Authors

MICHAEL GEERKEN is Chief Financial Officer at the Orleans Parish Criminal Sheriff's Office in New Orleans, Louisiana. He is the coauthor, with Walter Gove, of several articles dealing with sex, marital status, and the effect of children and work on the mental health of married men and women. He received his Ph.D. in Sociology from Vanderbilt University in 1979.

WALTER R. GOVE is Professor of Sociology and Anthropology at Vanderbilt University. Formerly Director of the NIMH Graduate Training Program, Professor Gove is an associate or consulting editor on such scholarly journals as *Women and Politics* and the *Journal of Health and Social Behavior*. He has published over 50 papers on topics ranging from suicide, sex roles, and racial equality to deviant behavior, social intervention, and labelling theory. His most recent work is **Deviance and Mental Illness** (Sage, 1982).